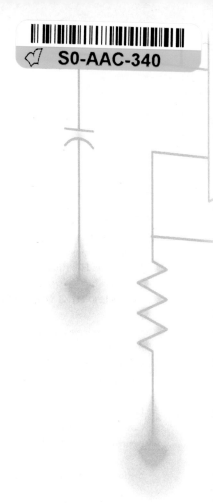

Schooling for the Knowledge Era

DAVID WARNER

ACER Press

First published 2006
by ACER Press
Australian Council for Educational Research Ltd
19 Prospect Hill Road, Camberwell, Victoria, 3124

Edited by Helen Bethune Moore
Cover and text design by Mason Design
Printed and bound by Shannon Books

National Library of Australia Cataloguing-in-Publication data:

Warner, David.
Schooling for the knowledge era.

Bibliography.
ISBN 0 86431 708 5.

1. Postmodernism and education. 2. Educational change.
3. Education - Philosophy. I. Title.

370.1

Visit our website: www.acerpress.com.au

Foreword

There are many books about what schools should be in the 21st century but there are few that tell the story with the authenticity that the reader will find in the pages that follow. David Warner is principal of a large co-educational school in Melbourne that has experienced a transformation under his leadership. He achieved what he advocated.

It is rare for those who lead the transformation of a school to have the opportunity to write about the experience. It is even more rare for them to do so in a manner that has meaning for other leaders and other communities. The stories that practitioners tell are mostly about their experience and often have limited value to those who face similar challenges in other places. This book is an exception. Experience at the ELTHAM College of Education is the helpful background that gives the story its authenticity. The bigger story is one that will help achieve the transformation of schools elsewhere in Australia and beyond.

I have had the good fortune to be associated with three principals who have written books and have such a capacity. The first was Jim Spinks, my co-author in the series on self-managing schools. His accomplishments as principal of a small and relatively isolated school in Tasmania were told in a story that transcended the setting and helped shape practice in systems of public education in several nations around the world. The second was David Loader, whose insights on the potential of technology to bring learning to a new level resulted in the transformation of Methodist Ladies' College in Melbourne. He drew on this accomplishment in writing *The Inner Principal*. It contributed to a more complete theory of leadership. I noted in my foreword that it was 'a guide and a reassurance to all who lead or aspire to lead in times of dramatic change' and that it made clear that 'success in the leadership of reform is as much a matter of discovering self as discovering strategy'. The outcome is a book that is timeless and universal in application. The third is David Warner in *Schooling for the Knowledge Era*. In many ways it subsumes the themes in the work of Jim Spinks and David Loader. What has been accomplished at Eltham College or what is advocated in the pages that follow can only be done in a self-managing school. The book also describes a personal journey for David Warner from the time he accepted the challenge and addressed the school at his first assembly in 2000 to the transformation that had been achieved by the middle of the decade.

Some readers or potential readers may be impatient at the thought of tackling one more book about the knowledge society. This book brings new insights to the topic, and they are refreshing. When David Warner writes about the importance of knowledge in an era of globalisation, he knows what he is talking about. I know of no other principal with his background in labour market research. His account of trends in the workforce and more generally in society is authoritative and understandable and therefore dependable. Moreover, he has done his homework. He writes about success at Eltham College, to be sure, but the book is packed with examples from a host of schools in several countries. Things are happening out there. The transformation is underway.

There is a sense of impatience running through the story. What must it take to demonstrate that schooling for the 21st century in a knowledge society must differ in important ways from schooling in the 19th and most of the 20th century in an industrial society? These differences extend to pedagogy, curriculum, technology, facilities, organisational structure, and connections between the school and the wider community. This is change on the scale of transformation, or as David Hargreaves expresses it, change that calls for a new 'education imaginary' to match the new 'social imaginary'. David Warner presents the challenge in the opening lines of the first chapter that draw on the stunning distinction between 'learners' and 'the learned' offered by Eric Hoffer. His impatience is evident in the opening lines of the last chapter: 'We are half a decade into the 21st century and most schools still have structures and curriculum that would be easily recognised back in 1950.' The good news for those who now have the book in their hands is that its pages provide a guide to how to achieve the transformation.

I define transformation as being significant, systematic and sustained change that results in high levels of achievement for all students in all settings, thus contributing to the well being of the individual and society. That change on this scale constitutes transformation is explained by the fact that the outcome has never been achieved across a nation at any time in the history of education. The reference to 'all students in all settings' implies that the learner is the most important unit of organisation—not the classroom, not the school, and not the school system. I wrote about this in *The New Enterprise Logic of Schools*. It is why personalising learning is a key strategy in achieving transformation. According to David Hargreaves, 'student voice' is one of the nine 'gateways' to personalising learning.

David Warner has written a convincing account of the importance of student voice and, consistent with the approach he has taken throughout, provides illustrations of how it is expressed and taken seriously in his school. I witnessed this at first hand when he agreed to give a presentation on personalising learning at a workshop of school leaders on the theme of 're-imagining the school'. The presentation was electrifying for it was given by two students from Eltham College who accompanied him and explained how it worked.

Professor Hedley Beare, whose 2001 book, *Creating the Future School*, set the ball rolling, has shaped my thinking on the topic and that of David Warner in important ways. *Schooling for the Knowledge Era* goes a long way to explaining and illustrating how such a future can be created. I am delighted that David Warner has cited one of the most powerful passages in recent writing in education in Hedley Beare's story about Angelica, reproduced in this book at the start of Chapter 3 and taken up in other places. No reader will forget the opening words: 'Hello, I am Angelica. I am five years old. I really don't have much of a past. In fact, I am the future.' Student voice is irresistible!

PROFESSOR BRIAN CALDWELL
Associate Director
Global International Networking for Educational Transformation

Contents

Acknowledgements

Young people and their interactions with the challenges of the global knowledge economy are an inspiration. This book came about because they challenged me to rethink their schooling. They have done that ever since I started teaching, but the world of the 21st century has created a new urgency for change. The young people of Eltham College of Education deserve my thanks for this book. Their teachers and parents deserve equal acknowledgement as people with courage, vision and determination to do the right thing by young people.

Many people encouraged me to write this book. The Board of Eltham College, particularly Chairman Chris Heysen, believed in telling the story. Steve Casey, from Hand Eye Communication, was a driving force behind the need to ensure that 'knowledge era schooling' as a concept was explained to a wider audience as a driver for change. David Loader, previous principal of Kinross Wolaroi, Methodist Ladies' College and Wesley, encouraged me back into schooling after a long absence and supported me as an innovator.

I would like to acknowledge Professor Hedley Beare whose writings always provided strong support for my actions, as well as Professor Brian Caldwell who believes in the importance of strong schooling and gave support to my writing.

My immediate colleagues supported this book in many direct and indirect ways: Iain Cowan, Greg King, Marg McCormack, Jenny Langmead, Sonia Van Hout and Phil Truscott. Particular acknowledgement needs to be given to Aine Maher, now Director, Teaching and Learning at the Association of Independent Schools of Victoria (AISV), a colleague with whom I prepared many papers that formed part of this book; Michele Owen who helped guide the communication in the writing, helped give it a parent sensitivity and assisted with the case studies; Dani Allgood, who managed much of the process and the communication with the many people involved in the book; and Tarecq Shehadeh, who assisted with early research. Joy Whitton, Managing Editor, ACER Press, read the manuscript and encouraged me and I thank her for her belief in its message.

Finally, much of the writing was done while I was on sabbatical in Europe. My wife, Debra, my son, Jake, and my daughter, Madison, accepted my 5 a.m. starts with creaky stairways and the days when I ignored them to write the first draft of this book. In addition, they put up with my life as a Principal/CEO. Thanks.

DAVID WARNER
August 2005

Permissions

The author gratefully acknowledges the permission to reproduce copyright material in this publication from the following sources: on p. 15 cartoon reproduced by permission of Rod Clement and Steve Casey, HandEye Communication; on p. 16 Figure 1 by permission of OECD; on pp. 22–3, 72–4, 141, 156 and 161 extracts by permission of Hedley Beare; on pp. 24, 62–3 and 76 extracts by permission of Malcolm Slade; on p. 33 table by permission of Harvard Business School Publishing; on pp. 94–6, 129, 130–1 and 132–3 extracts by permission of Aine Maher; on p. 97 architectural design by ClarkeHopkinsClarke; on pp. 104–5 extract by Sarah Browne; on p. 111 extract by permission of Chuck Salter; on pp. 136–7 by permission of Melinda Scash; student voices by permission of Eltham College of Education.

Case studies appear courtesy of Buckley Park College, Vic.; Buranda State High School, Qld; Cockatoo Montessori School, Vic.; Cramlington Community High School, Northumberland, UK; Dartford Grammar School, Kent, UK; Lauriston Girls' School, Vic.; New City School, Missouri, USA; Penrhos College, WA; Ringwood Secondary School, Vic.; and Wesley College, Clunes campus, Vic.

Introduction

In times of change learners inherit the earth;
while the learned find themselves beautifully equipped
to deal with a world that no longer exists.

Eric Hoffer, 1973

In a dramatically short space of time we have totally transformed our world, or if we don't have ownership of it, our world has been transformed for us. This change has moved us into a new era where all manner of interaction and communication, from the global to the individual, has been impacted. Consequently, many elements of our manner of operating in the world, whether in business, among friends, or in education have become outmoded. Indeed, our world has moved from the industrial era into the knowledge era and as educators of our present and future generations, we too must adapt in ways that meet the transformation of our times. As Elliott Eisner (2004) suggests, we must adapt in ways that make our schooling relevant to young people today because this will be the best means to prepare them for the future.

Let's review the macro elements of our world that have changed to give rise to the knowledge era.

- Perhaps the most global and pervasive change has been the advent of the Internet, with the most transparent changes being the way people communicate personally and in business, the pace with which information is transferred, and the exponential increase in our access to information.
- Rapid advances in information and communication technology mean we do business in a 'global economy' and the media now report on the 'global community' in which we live.
- The Australian labour market is changing, with a reduction in industrial era jobs and the growth of knowledge era jobs.

- The workplace is becoming more fluid, with the workforce required to be more autonomous and proactive in creating and responding to employment opportunities.

At the individual level these changes affect each of us differently, depending on our age.

But differences aside, we are all subject to the transformative effects of this new world. Just five years ago, 15 per cent of homes had Internet access. In 2005, the number of Australian homes with a young person under 15 years with Internet access has grown to 63 per cent. In growing numbers, adults and young people have mobile phones to communicate with others whenever and wherever they choose. We can talk, text, email and send photos by phone. Soon mobile phones will be able to do even more. Most of us have access to information at any time via the Web and increasingly through the use of handheld devices that can do all of the above.

When we narrow the focus to our young people in schools, we see a sophisticated group who are using any and all available methods to communicate and relate to one another, to acquire knowledge or access information. This is a far cry from the relatively few sources of information baby boomers (people born between 1946 and 1964) had available at the same age. Encyclopaedia sales staff still had a market in the 1990s—today they're selling mobile phones! The digital divide is less pronounced and, for young people, rarely an issue in terms of their access to information, new skills and challenging attitudes.

This book is written for parents and teachers wanting to better understand the world in which they are raising and educating their children and students respectively, and also wanting to ensure that schooling is in accord with the new world.

Our young people, whether in the classroom or in groups, have a different culture from the one that existed when older Australians were at school. This individual student and cultural difference is part of the knowledge era transformation and requires careful and systematic change from educators in order that we remain relevant and inspirational to our young people of the future.

My aim is to provide a well-considered perspective from which we can indicate how schooling can better serve our young people and their future. As a natural extension to this objective, this book also indicates the role schooling in Australia can play in creating a more competitive and appropriately skilled nation for the 21st century.

I have used a selected range of illustrations of schools and systems that have implemented or are implementing various changes associated with relevant knowledge era schooling. In addition to this, this book refers heavily to one school that made a commitment in 2000 to become a relevant school for young people of the 21st century: ELTHAM College of Education, Melbourne, Australia (hereafter referred to as Eltham College).

Eltham College is situated in the north-east of Melbourne in a designated 'green wedge' area, not open for residential or business development. It is a kindergarten to Year 12 co-educational, independent school of just under 1150 students. While it networks widely, it has no religious or other systemic affiliations. It is a public company owned by its parents and operates through a company board.

Creating a perspective for schooling in the knowledge era 1

I commenced as principal at Eltham College in Melbourne in 2000 and discovered that part of the school's tradition was to start the year with a whole-of-school assembly for 1200 young people from five to eighteen years. As a principal intent on making a difference and bringing about the changes needed to make schooling relevant and engaging for the 21st century, I agonised over this first public display. My previous position was in labour market research and policy development and this certainly increased my awareness of a massively changed global labour market, particularly for young people.

I had just moved with my family from Brisbane to Melbourne and we had been in our house for three weeks. Our kids were still coming to terms with leaving cousins and friends. My son (seven years old at the time) was wandering around the house with his Game Boy, often talking with his cousin in Brisbane to solve problems or share game strategies (they had a connector cable that had allowed them to share and game together). After watching this, I had a sudden realisation about what was happening: Jake and his cousin were demonstrating what I really wanted to say about young people and the new world.

I borrowed my son's Game Boy for the assembly. After welcoming everyone, I pulled his bright yellow Game Boy out of my pocket. A murmur of recognition swept the audience. Every student had used one or at least knew someone who used one. I directed student and staff attention to the fact that young people never needed an adult or teacher to show them how to use a Game Boy or solve any problems they may have had. They teach themselves and problem solve or work with their friends to find solutions and teach and learn with each other. Pretty amazing skills!

I talked to students about the skills they bring into school, the fact that they are highly capable learners, collaborators and teachers. I made a commitment that we, as a school, would work with them and together develop the skills they already had so that they would become self-directed and own their own learning. Later, I emphasised that their schooling should be about helping them become creators of the games rather than simply users. I spoke to them about Australian consumerism and how we were importers of knowledge products rather than creators and exporters of them.[1]

Our digital world

In 2003, we had free-to-air television and cable/satellite, a good choice of programs generally, and both video and DVD. Interactive DVD for most of us also is very recent (2002). Now, we have digital cable. Our television can be interactive; we have programs on demand, we can pause, play later, go back, use the Internet, shop online and so on. Do we realise that children under the age of fifteen will rarely know that this was a major change in our society? It will simply be part of their world but for some of us it will be a never-ending worry as to how we will use it.

Perhaps this is better illustrated by the Australian company Advanced Mobility Systems, which gives individuals the freedom to connect anytime and anywhere through a new generation of pocket computer handheld devices. They have a high-impact wireless application that integrates across and within business organisations to create greater efficiency and improve productivity. The applications are now being used in local council services to meet immediate repair needs, in real estate to provide alternatives to houses for inspection, in product sales in highly competitive areas such as coffee beans, and even in attendance procedures for school fieldtrips.

We now know more and have greater technology to manage information than ever before. According to international strategy and change guru Gary Hamel (2004), '12 per cent of what we now know in the world we learned in the last five years'. Over 6000 years of recorded history and 12 per cent of it known to us only in the last five years! Is it any wonder that our kids are different from us?

It was not long ago that written communication largely took the form of a letter. A letter could be received overnight, but generally it took several days or, if going overseas, it could take weeks. We planned time in which to write letters and rarely did we respond immediately to correspondence from friends or for business. In emergencies, we sent telegrams. Most of us, particularly those living in rural areas, dreaded receiving a telegram because it so often meant bad news. The clatter of the telex machine brought forth important information from another office that also had a telex machine. Telex machines were replaced by fax machines, which are still in use but decreasingly so.

Some 53 per cent of homes today have Internet connections; up from 16 per cent just five years ago, (ABS, 2004) and almost 100 per cent of workplaces have

---

1 In 1999, our exports of Information and Communication Technology (ICT) were less than 1% of GDP and our imports over 3%. Ireland's exports were 22%, South Korea 11%, UK 4%. New Zealand exported more ICT. If we consider the intellectual capital tied up in copyright, the copyright content in our trade was worth $1billion in export, but we actually imported $2.7 billion. (Source: OECD Database June 2001)

Internet connections. Written communication is immediate through email. Often the first thing that we do at work is check our emails, both work-related and private. Rarely do we set them aside, as with a letter, for another time to respond. Email is immediate and the sender expects an immediate response. In many businesses, including schools, the customer will be upset by a delayed response. At the very least they want immediate confirmation that you have received and read the email and are doing something about it. Not so long ago, our staff email server was infected with a virus and was out of operation for a week. People became angry that they were unable to send or receive messages. However, for one short week it seemed as if a lull occurred and people had more time. We realised, however, that our world had changed. We needed our emails to communicate, get things done and interact with our clients and customers.

The Australian Bureau of Statistics (2004) provides some very interesting information on young people and their Internet usage.

In the 12 months to April 2003, the Internet was accessed by 1 693 300 young people during or outside of school hours. This was 64% of all young people, aged 5–14 years, and 67% of young people who used computers. The proportion of females who accessed the Internet was slightly higher (66%) than the proportion of males who accessed the Internet (62%). Across the age groups, 21% of young people aged five years used the Internet, compared with 90% of 14-year-olds. Over half (61%) of the young people who accessed the Internet at home, did so more than once a week (824 800) and some (14% or 193 400) did so every day. The majority (70%) of young people who accessed the Internet at home every day were 12–14-year-olds, followed by 9–11-year-olds (23%), and 5–8-year-olds (7%).

The mobile phone with text messaging is now superseding email. It is more immediate because we carry our phones with us and increasing numbers of young people have them. The phone is an instrument for our immediate thoughts and we can use it almost anytime. Many young people in generation X (generally taken to be people born between 1964 and 1981) and generation Y (people born from 1982) use text messaging as their preferred means of communicating. Older people are still learning, although some have mastered the technique quickly and often use it. The mobile is now being integrated with personal computers and more of us are carrying all that we need to communicate and manage in a small portable device.

These are very simple illustrations of changes that have taken place in the first decade of the knowledge era. The changes that have occurred within the lifetime of anyone over 35 years old are almost beyond comprehension. Remember black and white television, the tone phone or vinyl records? Do you recall the mobile phones that were the size of bricks and powered by a car-sized battery? Yet today, we take for granted the fact that we have moved from an industrial society to a technological environment that we call the knowledge world. We only have to look in our homes and our workplaces to recognise the enormous changes that have occurred in such a short time.

The generational impact

What about the under-35s?

In 1980, people could not buy a personal computer (PC). Today, computers are readily available in most homes and workplaces and generally they are connected to the Internet. The under-35s also know that within six months of purchase, their computer and its software will have been superseded. There are few people under 35 who do not have to use a desktop computer or a laptop connected to the Internet for their daily work. Increasingly, we are using pocket PCs for all our out-of-office communication needs.

> The 'young' are older than they were several decades ago.
>
> Freeman, 1999

It is perhaps the under-20s who are most affected by this. They are caught on the cusp of change. On the one hand, their experiences involve continual change, taking risks, being independent, challenging authority and having access to more information than ever before, thanks to the Internet. If we are honest, we know that the conversations we can have with our twelve-year-olds are conversations we ourselves could not have had until we were well beyond school. My eleven-year-old son came with me to a school function in the city. On our 40-minute drive he challenged me on the existence of God and the value of religion. This was a conversation I had when I was in second year university.

On the other hand, these young people are faced with us—their parents and grandparents' generations and teachers. We have not yet understood what their world has become. Young people's skills are such that they should be seen as creative, demanding and challenging young leaders, but we tend to doubt these skills and attitudes and dominate them through our authority base in known subject knowledge and traditional schooling outcomes.

These young people, rightly, are confused between wanting to succeed in the traditional or familiar world of uniforms, exams and conformity, and the new world of self-management, risk-taking and independence. It is 14- to 15-year-olds, often young men, who are running software and website businesses, creating computer games and being recruited by schools and small businesses to set up their information technology (IT) systems. Many innovative schools employ these young men to challenge their IT security systems. These young people have put together self-learning packages online and manage various websites for their schools. They are clever beyond our reckoning.

Young people in the traditional mid-adolescent age range are facing enormous tensions. An Organisation for Economic Co-operation and Development (OECD) report (2001: 16) directs attention to a 'growing gap' between where schools are with their increasing concern about the control of children, and the private world where young people are more able to 'express choice, exercise autonomy, and work at their individual realisation' (Prout). The report suggests that it is increasingly difficult for schools to maintain legitimacy and sustain student motivation.

And then there are the under-12s. Five years ago, technology and computer games generally operated outside the Internet and few young people had continuous real-time access to the Internet. There was no X-Box, no Game Boy Advance. Today, these young people operate worldwide with games such as <http://www.runescape. com>. As I write, my son Jake is playing it with some 40 000 other users around the world. It is an interesting game: it involves collaboration and competition, lots of interaction and negotiation, teaching, learning and, of course, recreation. I asked Jake to look up something on the Internet for me (When was the first PC introduced?) and he said, 'Sure, but I am just helping another player, I will be about two minutes.' I stopped and watched and sure enough there was this game-interaction occurring between someone called Bashy and my son. Jake finished helping Bashy and then promptly found the answer (IBM in 1981).

Early writers have made very accurate predictions on the behaviours of young people with their use of emerging technologies. Rushkoff (1997), Tapscott (1998) and Turkle (1995) pointed to the easy familiarity that young people had with new technologies and how this would increase their expectations of what technology could do for them and what they could do with it. For many years now these young people have led the way, with adults sometimes having difficulty in following. Such familiarity is no longer confined to developed or Western societies. Most students in senior high school in Chinese cities (for example, Lu He and Nuilanshan in Beijing; Yuming in Dalian, Yu Cai in Shenyang) are regular surfers of the Internet and bring to school information attitudes never seen before by teachers. Rushkoff (1997) called them 'screenagers' with an enormous level of digital audacity.

Young people have such immediate and full access to the world and to the exponentially increasing world of information. My son, when asked to research a topic on the Internet for me, didn't say, 'Hang on Dad, I need to finish and get out of this and then I will look it up.' He just played with some keys and the mouse and had both going at once. My generation (perhaps also yours) would have feared, 'If I try to do this while the other is going, I'll lose it all!' There is a remarkable difference between us.

The global knowledge economy

Today's world is widely called 'the global knowledge economy'. Enabled by rapid changes in Information and Communication Technology (ICT)—mainly the Internet and high-speed access—the global economy is dominated by knowledge processes and knowledge products that can be enabled, developed and delivered through the Internet. Stock markets, for example, that dominate the world economy are no longer local or national despite the names associated with them—New York, Tokyo, Hong Kong, London, Frankfurt, Sydney and so on. There are few business corporations that are not global and enabled by new ICT, particularly the Internet. Very few small businesses are not directly influenced by what is happening around the globe. That influence is immediate and comes through the Internet.

We use the word 'knowledge' to describe our economy because it sums up what we have when we access information and manipulate it so that it is useful, productive, meaningful and valuable. Much of what we rely on today is the product of taking information and manipulating it or adding value to it by using knowledge processes: critical thinking, problem solving, collaborating and teaming, innovation and so on. However, such processes are enabled by ICT and the Internet and through our capacity to work together using this technology.

The global knowledge economy is in stark contrast to the era that preceded it. That era was best typified by traditional manufacturing, specialised but routine job tasks, supervised work and controlled workplaces. People most often had jobs for life and company loyalty was expected from both the employer and the employee. Young people could get permanent jobs on leaving school, often around fifteen years of age.

The knowledge economy supplanted much of this and took away the traditional security of the industrial world. In fact, 1975–2000 was a period of massive change and social dislocation in the industrialised world as it crashed through from industrial manufacturing to smart technology and smart jobs. The youth labour market changed enormously with few permanent jobs available and more and more jobs requiring further education and training. The youth labour market became casual and part-time, and combined work and study. More permanent work did not come until young people were in their mid to late twenties.

Peter Drucker, the American management guru, sums up the knowledge era very well when he says:

> In a few hundred years, when the history of our time will be written from a long-term perspective, it is likely that the most important event historians will see is not technology, not the Internet, not e-commerce. It is an unprecedented change in the human condition. For the first time—literally—substantial and rapidly growing numbers of people have choices. For the first time, they will have to manage themselves. And society is totally unprepared for it.

Drucker, 2000

This is the real difference between the industrial era and the knowledge era. Today, people have to be more responsible for their own lives and manage their own life–work expectations and experiences.

In the past, a generally secure workplace, assisted by governments, took much of the responsibility for us. We did not need much initiative or creativity to hold a job. Jobs were often very routine and most work and workers were supervised. There was a management and supervision hierarchy in which each worker's level of autonomy and decision-making was well defined. Workers did not take too many, if any, risks. Innovation, where it existed, belonged largely to higher-level management. In fact, management often felt inadequate and affronted if those they supervised put forward innovations. Qualities sought in the workforce were things such as reliability, the ability to work with minimal direct supervision, punctuality, hard work and loyalty to the company.

Today however, the essence of success is risk-taking and innovation because the service and knowledge jobs of today demand higher-order skills and individual responsibility for decision-making. If you are aged between 25 and 65 years old, you know this because it is affecting your life.

If you are over 45, you are likely to be told that you are too old to change, to train and to become innovative and you are worried about being able to work long enough to ensure a comfortable retirement (if you are not made redundant first).

If you are under 45, you know that to succeed and to maintain your job or your business you have to be innovative, take risks and continue to learn and change. You have to be a life-long learner.

If you are under 25, the new world is yours and I suspect you just wish we would let you get on with it, rather than stifling you with our industrial age practices and attitudes.

The education dilemma

The world of schooling is in turmoil: it faces an education dilemma. It is caught in the middle between industrial era expectations and knowledge world realities, challenges and opportunities.

Its clients, the young people in schooling today, are the 'knowledge era kids'. They are not of the industrial era. Their world is of learning, teaming, teaching, risk-taking and having fun. Add to this their rapidly growing access to information through the Internet, their awareness through exposure to multimedia and media and their willingness to take risks and we have a different generation—a generation that has changed completely and whose world is difficult for their parents and grandparents' generations to understand. It is easy for people to say, 'But every generation has been like this!' Most generations have been able to say, 'In my day, we . . .' Today however, we recognise that young people (Generation Y) have access to information and exposure to the world that gives them knowledge, skill and attitudes that are completely different from those of previous generations. No other generation has seen war and terrorism on television as it happens, or has been able to communicate and play games in real time with people 20 000 kilometres away. No other generation has had access to new films and music on or before their release or been able to get almost any information they want at the touch of a button. (And yes, this generation does need assistance in the ethics of using Internet information. This generation is also at risk of being desensitised through overexposure to the realities of the world and this adds another dimension to the need to transform schooling.)

This level of access became even more acutely obvious to me, when on a recent trip to China it became apparent that students worldwide are regularly accessing the Internet and learning exciting multimedia skills. However, their teachers were teaching multimedia in lock-step fashion as if the students had no skill. Few Chinese principals, teachers and parents of students in middle and senior schools are not aware of the influence of global access to information on their students. In the United Kingdom, there is perhaps more recognition of a need to change schooling than in any other country. However, they are focusing on change through school leadership, through teaching and through traditional subject areas as shown through the schools associated with the Specialist Schools Trust.

Similar approaches to the mass teaching of multimedia in China are employed in Australia and in most international schools where control, management and teacher knowledge authority are top priorities. Teacher unions and, indeed, some governments and would-be governments are positioning discipline as a major item for political agendas.

Schools and teachers throughout the world are largely out of step with today's kids. They are failing to create the learning opportunities that the new era and its young people demand. They often do not create the fun in learning required to really engage young people. This engagement is needed to help develop a positive disposition towards life-long learning, that is, self-direction in learning. We really want young people to love their schooling experiences because without this how can we expect them to value both learning and earning throughout their lives? To love learning, they must have fun! The OECD report (2001) reinforces this when it points out that there is an increasing gap between the school and the world of young people, which means that it is increasingly difficult to motivate young people.

The industrial school model is one based on control and authority. Neither of these is concerned with learning, the development of self-discipline or self-management, or having fun and getting to love learning. At best, it is about adults and schools trying very hard to maintain their control over young people and their emerging world and to teach them subject knowledge that has passed its use-by date. For example, there are no current subject disciplines that do or can teach emotional intelligence, that is, for young people to develop self-awareness and be able to manage their relationship with the world around them. This is despite the fact that we know that the world has changed so dramatically.

Many adults operate in a culture of denial where they do not acknowledge the world of young people, but rather try to hang onto their own world and world views. This was brought home to me recently at a business breakfast. A young-ish solicitor questioned the new world for young people by suggesting, 'Yes, the world has changed, but schools shouldn't because we need discipline, tradition and certainly, the tertiary entrance results.' The solicitor had recognised the denial and the difficulties between the two worlds, but was not ready to admit that change was needed if schooling was to engage young people.

Conflict in schools

Young people in schools today are living and often creating a new world of their own outside school. They are leaders and innovators, but too often schools do not see or value these skills in them. Rather, schools see the attitudes and skills of young people as challenging authority, and place discipline (order, management and control) at the top of the agenda. For the last 30 years we can compare these traditional schools to a battlefield, with structure and control as the ultimate prize. These schools represent the industrial world's continuing control over young people, trying to maintain them within the old world of traditional curriculum, assessment and credibility.

The new world of the knowledge era, however, is not simply computers and technology. It is how we work together, young people and adults, and how we use all the tools at our disposal to become learners and workers. This includes computers and the Internet as major enabling tools—they are key elements of a new literacy. We need to move beyond the 20th-century arguments about 'the digital divide'. Computers and how they are accessed is not the point. The point is information, communication and attitude. The number of personal computers in a school is not the issue. The issue is whether the school has the culture for young and old to collaborate, sharing their skills and talents.

I am not suggesting a schooling conspiracy against young people, even though it may seem that way. We have an ageing, conservative teaching population who still manage, indeed control, the newer, novice teachers who themselves are in conflict over what they and schools should be doing. Teachers have always espoused middle-class values and have largely done their traditional job of passing on the culture or, indeed, of socialising young people into the accepted culture of the adult world.

Many teachers have difficulty in understanding the world of young people because it is far removed from their world. Newer teachers are more in touch with the world view of young people, but the environment of schools makes it very difficult for them to make a difference.

The world from which young people are coming is a threatening world for many adults, and particularly that of older teachers whose work has depended on their being able to manage and control young people within schools through their greater knowledge and authority. Most teachers would recognise that they do this with considerable caring and a great commitment to teaching young people. It is not a deliberate strategy, but rather one gained through experience and a belief in the familiar. Many principals (ageing faster than their teachers) are resistant to change, often because they do not want the anxiety of change in their last few working years.

Schools often use controlling language and very little of it concerns the new world of young people. We use the words 'child', 'children' and 'students'—some use 'pupil'—to describe young people, even 17- and 18-year-olds finishing school. The terms clearly conjure the image of an immature person with limited capability in terms of thinking and decision-making. Yet, up to 60 per cent of eight-year-old girls are reported to be pubescent and the awareness they have of the world is years ahead of that of previous generations. Today, 11- to 12-year-olds start conversations and question issues that even 10 years ago few students in senior school would have raised in serious discussion with older people. We use terms such as 'teacher' and 'student', clearly implying that the latter learns from the former. We still use 'pastoral care' as a term relating to how we look after young people and provide for their social, emotional and spiritual needs. The term is religious and implies doing something to protect or guide. Again, this emphasises what we *do* to young people. It's not about helping them to learn to manage their lives.

Parent attitudes

One of the difficult things for parents is to question schooling in relation to their own children's experiences. For many parents, there is a sense of security and comfort in feeling that school will give their children the knowledge, values and experiences that they had as young people. This is despite their knowing that these, save perhaps some of the values, have retained little relevance to their own life and work experiences, particularly over the past 10 to 15 years.

Parents know that their children have attitudes, life experiences and skills that are in conflict with schooling. They know that they let their young teenagers go to parties and out with their friends. Yet, they still accept, even ask for, detentions, discipline and punishments in the belief or with a perception that these things will ensure the right schooling outcomes for their children. It is bizarre, but understandable. We are in a very busy world and I suspect that often we do not share our thoughts, perceptions or observations with other parents or adults. Perhaps if we did we would discover that what our own children are doing is pretty similar to what other young people are doing. More than this, we might even be impressed by their enormous skills, achievements and access to information about the world. For the first time we might even wonder whether their attitude is because they are growing up (remember, this process is starting very early) or because they are bored with school and angry at not being recognised for what they bring to learning, or more to the point, because schools are trying to suppress their energy and risk-taking.

I am amazed at the parents of boys, for example, who actually support schools' disciplining their young men for attitude problems to learning while these same young men are leading the new world in their use of modern technology. These young men are rejecting, in different ways and at varying levels, the traditional subject disciplines and teaching–learning processes because they are ahead of these subjects and approaches through their own skills and access to information and in their attitudes. I recognise that it is difficult to generalise, but my experience and research suggests that I am correct in thinking this way rather than perceiving the attitudes of young people as being simply negative. Is it any wonder that young people develop a strong antipathy towards school and learning?

I worry that schooling is stifling the very creativity, innovation and leadership we need from young people to compete successfully in this new global knowledge economy and that this, unfortunately, is being supported by parents, media and government policy. Often this is because the whole issue of the knowledge era young person has been put into the 'too hard basket'.

Taking the leap

Australia, with its rapidly ageing population and a declining population of under-18s, does not have the numbers to continue to educate a chosen few as innovators to lead us to success. We need our total population to be thinkers, risk-takers, innovators and entrepreneurs. On a global scale, for example, Europe, with its union of smaller populations, has recognised the changes associated with the global knowledge economy, and is positioning itself far more positively than the current world knowledge economy power, the United States. The same can be said of China.

Changing schooling can be seen as a risky business. For many parents, schools represent one thing that can be seen as a stabilising influence in a confusing, complex and transformed world. School educators hold on to what parents believe they valued in their own schooling: values, religion, discipline, traditional academic subjects, liberal education and entry to university.

The industrial era school is now a relic, focused on controlling talent. The knowledge era school works with young people to release and enhance their considerable talents.

This book is about the knowledge era school. It will look at the society and economy that created the culture for such schooling, describe the change processes that are needed to develop relevant knowledge era schooling and then describe the knowledge era school itself, how it works and the outcomes that can be expected from it.

Look at young people and the world they live in. They have such wonderful attitudes and talents. We need to transform our schools so that they support, work with and grow our young people with their own positive world views for the 21st century. To do this we need to make a commitment to genuine transformation. This book helps us to understand this commitment. It is about all schools: public, independent and Catholic. They each comprise similar young people who share attitudes, skills, talents and dreams. These young people can do without our adult perceptions of school sectors. I suspect they would just like all of us to make their schooling relevant.

The dilemma is exacerbated by constant political and media challenges over standards. Schooling for the knowledge era needs also to redefine standards for the 21st century. These standards have to relate to the knowledge era, not the industrial era. We need to embrace standards that demand schooling experiences and outcomes that reflect 21st-century literacy, emotional intelligence, disposition and skill for learning for life, and the ability to self-manage. We can, as situations demand, incorporate traditional standards as they relate to other avenues for learning, for example, university.

In this book I try to focus us on the present and future. Too often the issue of standards is about the past. We cannot afford to apply the principles and standards of an era that has passed. Adults today must recognise that schooling needs to cater for all young people. The adult memory is of the past and is often of schooling that catered for 20–30% of students that went on to university. This is an industrial mindset and we must be careful not to lock 21st century young people into it.

Originally published in the *Australian Financial Review*

Our knowledge world

Since the 1980s (and some would say much earlier), we have experienced a world increasingly dominated by global corporations. Acquisition tentacles have spread across national boundaries at a rapid rate, and now national agendas are heavily influenced by corporate objectives. Once business recognised the potential power of the Internet and emerging ICT, it took less than a decade for this group to make technology user-friendly and the Internet an integral and mandatory component for anyone wanting to participate in business.

Personal computers, available from 1981, were simply powerful tools for analysis and calculation. It was the Internet that made the difference. Suddenly, there were no boundaries at all in the developed world to accessing, sharing and sending information, to global stock markets and global trading, to ensuring that those who needed to know your detailed—and sometimes confidential—information had it within seconds of your sending it via email or providing a link to a website.

As a function of these millions of new connections coming online at the same time, knowledge has become productive and valuable and the predominant global commodity. It can be developed and traded quickly and is what we now describe as the core product of the global knowledge economy. A significant feature of wealth, both corporate and individual, has become intellectual capital applied successfully in the marketplace. The chief product of this economy is knowledge and, if you had ever wondered about Australia's balance of trade in knowledge, we are currently in deficit. We are largely consumers of knowledge products and services, not creators (see Figure 1).

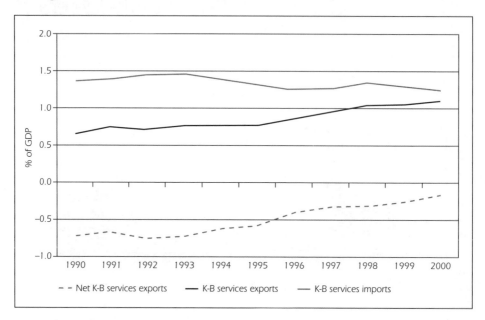

Figure 1: Trade (Net Exports) in Australian knowledge-based services, 1990–2000

Source: Calculations derived from OECD Statistics on International Trade in Services, OECD/Eurostat 2001
©OECD *Preliminary OECD 2000 data

The phrase 'knowledge era' derives from the term 'global knowledge economy', which is regularly used to describe the globalised nature of business, banking and finance, television networks, telecommunications, tourism and many other industries. However, it is better defined in terms of the new economics in which intangibles, such as information and intellectual capital, have been enabled by information technology to become the valuable drivers of international commerce. According to Goldfinger (1996), the shift from material goods to intangibles is a defining feature of the new economy. It is what traditional economic theory has difficulty dealing with and why it is becoming increasingly necessary to look to evolutionary economic approaches that have a far greater focus on how technology, innovation and learning, intellectual capital and loyalty are at the core of modern economic transformation (DETIR, 1999). Today's reality is that 'knowledge matters for economic performance' (Quah, 1998).

Availability of information is now growing at an exponential rate and is being used to create knowledge, knowledge processes and knowledge product. The term 'knowledge processes' can also be called 'knowledging' and refers to the process or action of working with information and creating knowledge. Young people, as students, are continuously engaged in knowledging as they negotiate and sift through a plethora of information of various quality (writing, playing, reading, creating, making sense of television), and now increasingly so is the workforce. We are moving, for example, to virtual teams in global and national organisations, where people engage in collaborative work and knowledging via online conferencing and email. As our business leaders realised from the outset, advances in communications technology mean a talented global team can be at work around the clock.

'Knowledge product' refers to an outcome of knowledging. It might be a new welfare system developed after intensive web-based research for relevant international comparisons, or a specific product such as an education course or software. Today's surgeons can perform miraculous keyhole surgery via a computer screen thanks to an ingenious knowledge product and can collaborate in the process internationally. Information technology (IT) software is a good example of working with information and creating new knowledge and new ways of seeing and doing things. Value adding is another example that Australia has discovered only over the past decade. Once we simply shipped raw materials and primary produce to international markets. Having recognised what others have been doing with our materials, we are more focused on adding the value before shipping, as for example, in meat export. However, there are many areas where it is now too late for us to do the value adding.

It is staggering to conceptualise that in the past 15 years more history has been recorded than in the entire recorded history of the world. Telecommunication advances allow us to experience history in real-time. Television crews wait in the desert sand dunes before a pre-dawn attack commences, cycling fans around the globe followed Lance Armstrong's record-breaking seventh Tour de France as it happened, a ground-breaking new product is launched simultaneously worldwide with an accompanying advertising campaign, or the unfolding first election result in a newly democratised nation is monitored by media around the globe. The knowledge era ultimately implies a boundary-free environment where the flow of ideas, collaboration and commerce occur without limitation.

It is hard to have perspective when nothing has prepared us for this fluid and speed-of-thought environment. These days, it is the principles by which we live rather than traditionally slow-moving external cues such as employment and now-defunct job security that allow us to feel that we are in control of our own lives. Even the most progressive-thinking parents who want their children to learn to deal with the knowledge world are grappling with the complexities it creates. How do we manage our ten-year-olds' access to more information than has ever been available before through the Internet? More importantly, how do we manage to teach them how to use it wisely and ethically?

Connecting public conscience through the Internet

The response to the most recent Iraq war is a classic example of connecting public conscience through the Internet. Through email and SMS text messaging, protest groups in the United States, Europe, Australia and other locations were organising mass protests before the war even began. The US-based virtual organisation, MoveOn.org, is one example of an online presence that informed small protest groups nationwide that their anti-war sentiments were not isolated pockets of protest, but part of a larger movement that was growing in strength on a daily basis.

After the horrors of the Spanish train bombing in Madrid in 2004, organisers of protest against the government used SMS messages to call in large numbers of protestors on the eve of the election. They helped bring down the government at the next day's election.

Public conscience is so well connected through our technology that 'divide and conquer' can no longer work for controlling interests. It represents a complete shift in societal dynamics when online conversations provide anyone with a network to like-minded individuals.

This is an age of much greater freedom of thought and information for young people through 'cyber travel'. This has led to greater freedom of action and this, in itself, is scary for parents.

There are many implications, but at the thin end of the wedge, the knowledge era leaves its participants little time for reflection. When events occur in real-time, the present and the future are being shaped and re-shaped far more rapidly because of the greater number of participants at any one time.

Where Australia fits . . .

> ... if Australia is to remain globally competitive and, indeed, if it is to avoid becoming globally irrelevant, more and more of its workers must be able ... to participate positively and opportunistically in global labour markets. That is to say, they must be employed ... in those occupations that are essentially conceptual/creative in nature, and/or in those conceptual/technical occupations that either support or are allied to them ... The onus is very much, therefore, on Australia's education and training system ...
>
> Maglen, Monash University Centre for Economics of Education and Training, 2001

Australia is a small player in the rapidly developing global knowledge economy. The entrepreneurial and risk-taking nature that is associated with the character of Australians has the potential to make disproportionately large contributions and reap significantly larger rewards per capita in the future than many other countries. The knowledge era economy supports countries that are smart enough to have innovative, self-directed, and entrepreneurial knowledge workers who can thrive in a fast-moving, changing environment.

One area where Australia is making attempts to take commercial advantage of the global knowledge economy is as a major exporter of education, largely in the sense of international students coming to Australia for school or university and, to a lesser degree, setting up education opportunities in other countries, mainly in Asia. Our education 'knowledge product' is good, but how long this will remain so is a big question because of exchange rates and competition from the rest of the education world. Those who master the knowledge era education concept of moving quickly, without the illusion that the market will turn to traditional sources of academic knowledge, will reap the most benefit. Singapore is now the regional leader in education export, particularly to China. It is making major inroads into Australia's market.

Workforce transformation in Australia is still in its early stages. We are moving beyond recognising that the labour market and the nature of jobs have changed to being proactive in planning for it. Europe commenced the process around the time of their first Education White Paper, published in 1994. The UK is engaged in massive and wonderfully challenging and invigorating transformation for the right reasons. Smaller countries in Asia, led by Malaysia and Singapore, also started transforming their economies at the same time. Today, Hong Kong's production is in knowledge products and importantly, their education system is recognising this fact. This past producer of labour-intensive products is now a knowledge producer. Japan is also in the process of transforming its schooling. Members of China's Central Committee are reviewing its schooling and university systems, particularly its college entrance examinations. Australia's danger is not in change itself, but in failing to match this rate of transformation.

There is strong support for the notion that the workplace of the industrial era, as it existed more than 15 years ago, is significantly different from the knowledge era workplace that exists today, and that the differences will be even more pronounced in the future (ABS Census of Population and Housing, 2001). These workplace differences are characterised by:

- An exponential increase in the use and functionality of information and communication technology. The shift to the use of web-based communication by business has ensured that the barriers traditionally preventing individuals anywhere around the world from communicating for work or leisure no longer exist.
- The movement of the majority of nations to participate in the global marketplace—what is commonly termed 'globalisation'—has created new horizons to market a good or service, with a commensurate increase in work opportunities for knowledge workers internationally.
- Australia's traditional business structures and hierarchies are modelling for what is now a far more fluid and dynamic working environment. Influences including merit-based awards, flexible work hours and the need for cost-efficient business management have led to outsourcing, consideration of family values and life–work balance, and sustained economic growth.

Enter the knowledge workers

They need to be multi-skilled, they have to have the capacity to analyse, problem solve and recognise they will not have a single career path. It's very different from the industrial economy where you prepared some students for manufacturing jobs, and others for the professions, and so schools split the curriculum into vocational and academic. Today's workers need to be multi-skilled, and I think schools are grappling with that complexity.

Alan Reid, University of South Australia, Education Professor, 2003

In this new environment, the individuals who thrive in the knowledge era workplace are the ones who can make informed decisions based on available information and can relatively quickly provide meaningful solutions for a public or private entity in the marketplace. The knowledge era workplace is the closest experience Australians have had to the workings of the free market.

Within Australia, the offshore movement of manufacturing, together with the rise of knowledge-based services, is a telling trend to Australia's place in the new globalised economy. It is having a marked effect on enterprises and employment, particularly for young people (up to 26 years old) who are performing historically higher rates of casual, part-time and contract work (ABS, 2001; Mangan, 1998). A steadily growing percentage of young people in the workforce must be comfortable moving where opportunity takes them, which can commonly include either interstate or overseas positions where they are learning to work effectively in an international market where skills are highly transferable.

For young people, the choice of professions is rapidly changing, with significant numbers of current occupations available that were not in existence five years ago. The newest careers include a greater focus on individuals as small business operators, acting as contractors with new knowledge and skills to sell. The world of multimedia is creating new types of work all the time. Every form of employment, however established, has been directly or indirectly transformed and influenced by the knowledge era.

Electronic information services, including software development, have been significant areas of employment growth throughout the Western world, China, India and Japan over the past ten years. While jobs in the direct IT sector have declined, those in all other industries that require IT as part of their operations have seen enormous growth. Print publishing is another good example, as is paper-based archiving, once a large provider of jobs, but which now has virtually disappeared to be replaced by electronic publishing and archiving, again meaning fewer jobs.

This, of course, is at the very heart of the changes. Traditional jobs are being replaced by newer, smarter, technologically enabled jobs, but there are fewer of them. Industries that have created employment include the financial services sector, computing services, motion pictures and multimedia, among others. The travel industry and postal services are other examples of sectors where the knowledge economy has changed the nature of employment. The Internet has greatly expanded the market in travel and created a decline in traditional travel industry jobs. However, tourism has created new knowledge worker jobs in the services industry, for example in resort services or leisure and recreation.

It is entirely understandable then that the qualities individuals must develop to succeed in the knowledge era environment include the ability to:

- think and act like an independent contractor (even if they find themselves from time to time working in a large corporation)
- readily adjust and see opportunity in sudden change
- collaborate so that required services can be delivered with flexibility and without commitment to unnecessary cost structures
- willingly learn on an ongoing basis for personal and professional improvement
- incorporate new technology into one's work or life if there is a real benefit to the quality of life or work performed.
- work in more fluid environments with less structure and management
- strive for innovation and creativity in work and play.

Summary

The knowledge era with its unprecedented change has transformed our world. Our knowledge era world is not knowledge in the traditional sense of subjects or disciplines, but the skill and maturity to quickly access information and use it to create knowledge and opportunity.

The labour market of the new global knowledge economy rewards knowledge workers who can self-learn, be innovative and risk-takers, can communicate quickly and effectively, problem solve and adapt to rapid change.

With this understanding of the rapid and pervasive transformation that characterises the knowledge era, we can turn to the implications for the education of our young people in schools.

3 | The rationale for change

Best practice schooling creates opportunities for
individuals based on their natural strengths
and aptitudes. It has a culture that accepts and works
with young people so that their skills are acknowledged
and they have the disposition and skill to deal
with the world as it is.

The student of today

I am the future's child

Hello, I am Angelica. I am five years old. I really don't have much of a past. In fact, I am the future.

You need to understand what I am learning to believe, how I think about my future, what my world view is. You and I both want me to be a success in the world which I will enter as an adult and which I will be responsible for. In future days I will admire you for being able to look forward with me and help me define what I need to learn.

My world is already very different from the one you have grown up in.

On present life expectancy, I will live until I am over 80. I will be alive and well into the 2070s and my children will live to see the twenty-second century. Can you imagine what the world will be like for them?

During my lifetime, a planet-wide economic system will operate, controlled … by business networks and regional centres of trade like Singapore, Bangkok, Mexico City, Los Angeles … Sydney …

… When I complete my twelve years of schooling, every one of my classmates will be expected to undertake some form of post-school training … In-service training, retraining for a different occupation, professional development and continuous study or learning will be facts of life for my generation throughout our lives.

… All these things I have talked about are the raw materials I use to weave my life together. I want to be hopeful and happy and comfortable about my future. It doesn't help me if adults keep telling me gloomy things about the future. Education is all about hope, isn't it? Your schooling was.

… Most of all I want to be wise about what to believe about me and my world. I want to know what the wisest people on earth believe. I want to know how to be a success with my life … My school teachers are very important to me because they tell me how to deal with the future—the long, long future.

… So, do you know what to teach me? Do you know what I need to learn? And do you know how to teach me? Are you confident that you can design a curriculum which will equip me to live in my world?

… My name is Angelica. I am five years old. And, I am sitting in your classroom today.

Professor Hedley Beare, 2001

This visionary description of the student that educators must help to prepare for the workplace of 20 years from now captures the essence for the impetus of knowledge era schooling transformation. It is not simply a matter of defining the knowledge, skills and capabilities young people need to be innovators. Rather, it is a matter of recognising their talents and already developed skills of learning, collaborating and teaching and ensuring that they have the environment in which these can flourish and grow. Schools that still control young people cannot effectively provide an environment for young people to be creative, innovative or entrepreneurial.

Students today are remarkable exploiters of technology and the multimedia society in which they live. The skills they possess in these areas coupled with the enormous information they can access make them extraordinarily different from previous generations. There is confidence, a great sense of enjoyment, considerable collaboration with their peers, creativity and problem-solving capability. They can differentiate sub-cultures within their music and culture, can critique fashion and discriminate media hype and advertising. They explore film, video and DVD and can create interesting sound systems and amateur film. They can enjoy and analyse sport and sporting personalities. They have a fair handle on themselves and do not see too much wrong with being 'me' focused, but within the context of supporting their mates. They can distinguish between right and wrong and make informed choices when they want to.

These great attributes start early. They seek help from their mates and problem solve with them. They connect their games and collaborate. Most can save and direct their purchasing to what they want. They demonstrate as highly disciplined learners, able to focus, give time-to-task, give effort and achieve. We need to move our thinking, and hopefully that of the media, from the negative portrayal of young people. Unfortunately, there does appear to be an agenda that wants society to see the negative, in fact to be afraid of what might happen. Michael Crichton, in his novel *State of Fear* (HarperCollins, 2004) has his characters discussing this and one says:

In reality, for the last 15 years we have been under the control of an entirely new complex … I call it the political-legal-media complex. The PLM. And it is dedicated to promoting fear in the population—under the guise of promoting safety. (pp. 455–6)

In an author's message he goes on:

The current near-hysterical preoccupation with safety is a waste of resources and a crimp on the human spirit, and at worse an invitation to totalitarianism. Public education is desperately needed. (p. 571)

Although the media often suggests society should fear youth, most young people have a social conscience and are pretty capable outside the school and classroom. Many, however, react against learning situations that involve their putting away their talents, skills and interests and taking on 'stale classroom corners'. Their living and learning is fast-paced, just like their computer games, music and sport. Their attention is multifaceted, but often brief as they move from one activity or screen to the next. Having to focus on one area of often seemingly irrelevant curriculum for 30 to 60 minutes does not sit comfortably with the lives they lead or their perceptions of the world around them.

It's all right… school. It's just if it wasn't boring and strict, and they made it a little bit more fun, the teachers relaxed a little bit more.

Slade, 2001

And what of those young people just starting their school years? We now have five-year-olds who can install and play quite sophisticated computer games and use sophisticated learning tools on CDs; seven-year-olds who look first on the Internet for the information they want; fifteen-year-olds downloading films produced solely for Internet users. Ten-year-olds make decisions about which provider offers the best search engine for what they are seeking. Many of us might say they are wasting time and resources. From our perspective, playing Internet games may well be a waste of time with no relationship to our interests or use as knowledge. However, think about all of this in terms of the powerful learning tools and sophisticated techniques they are learning and developing. When they strike a problem or cannot do something, they collaborate with a friend or find a solution. Often what they are doing is shared and collaborative: they are teaming. Think about the capacity to apply this to other work, and to learning. Think about young people's skills in communicating and their use of email and SMS texting. How many have hotmail addresses and are having real-time conversations online after school, or indeed during school during less than exciting classes? How many who say they don't like writing actually have no problem sending emails to the next-door classroom or around the world?

A group of senior students at a seminar worked to make their point:

> I am a child of the knowledge era. Information and communication technology has been ever present during my life. I have technology skills that rival those of my parents and many of my teachers. I'm not afraid of new technology. I adapt to it as it continues to improve.
>
> The Internet is my favourite tool. There is no limit to the information that I can access. Sometimes, I need help to work out what to do with all this information, how to use it to learn and create my own knowledge.
>
> Every day, I can make choices about what I want to discover. I also need to make informed choices about where I am going in my life; choices that will lead me to undertaking many different careers.
>
> I can do things for myself. I can research school projects, shop online, join a game with players all over the world, email my friends and make my own web site.
>
> I work together with my friends to solve problems. I understand that technology connects me not just to my friends but also to the world. This connection provides me with new opportunities to work with others and share ideas at home, at school and in future employment.
>
> I have the freedom to explore the whole world!

Given the opportunity, this is the environment in which young people will naturally thrive if schools would recognise and reflect their knowledge era thinking.

> It's not teacher-to-student communication, but person-to-person communication. It's not that one is necessarily smarter but rather power struggle doesn't exist. The teacher's role is to use their much broader experience to set up an environment where younger people can call on their natural curiosity and intelligence. The adult's role is to ensure that the younger person goes through that discovery process thoroughly and matches curriculum requirements.
>
> Gavin, Year 12

Evidence for change

Research conducted in 1997 on workers-in-training and school graduates at university and TAFE (Warner, Christie and Choy, 1998) found that some 70 per cent of the Australian workforce and Australian undergraduates were ill-prepared for flexible delivery of further learning; that is, it was evident they were not self-directed as learners, and uncomfortable with the idea of learning outside a teacher-directed classroom. Further, students in the sample almost entirely took their cues as to what they should learn from someone else, such as an employer or parent, rather than deciding what they needed or wanted for themselves to enhance their lives and work. It was startling to discover many simply had no opinion about their own learning at that time or for the future. Critically, the evidence showed they did not have the disposition to be self-directed. They were not motivated as learners, let alone as life-long learners.

The big question, therefore, was how could a workforce actually succeed in the knowledge era and the global knowledge economy where job and skill change were givens if they could not learn flexibly for themselves? There was little evidence in the research of people learning flexibly or seeing the need to learn flexibly. The implications of the enormous changes in the global labour market, it seemed, had not registered with the sample group. For the majority of students, this is where second-ary schools can play a seminal role in shaping the disposition of young Australians and their attitudes to learning.

In a 2004 Youth Vision for Schooling Conference held in Melbourne, young leaders said in relation to post-school:

POST-SCHOOL LIFE
Students' lives do not stop after they receive their ENTER (tertiary entrance) score. That is why schools need to emphasise the importance of post-school life. The world of work is ever changing, therefore, it is extremely important that schools are equipping their students with the skills that they need to not just survive in this world, but to excel and be leaders. This change also demands the need for competent life–work/career counsellors to ensure that students are not limited with their options. Students need to be aware that there are many options other than university. Schools need to change with the times. It is as simple as that. If we are to move forward into the future, it is pivotal that our schools provide students with the facilities and the opportunities to acquire the skills to be adaptable to change and become life-long learners.

This is a powerful statement from young people who have recognised the need for schooling change.

During the late 1990s, academics were well aware of what was about to come. Savage (1996: 245) put it bluntly and, in most instances in education, we have still to hear the message:

We have two choices: stay with the industrial era mindset and computerise our steep hierarchies, or reform our thinking towards the integration that is possible through human networking. The first choice will not overcome our organisational bankruptcy. The second choice will add value to past investments and increase future investments.

A futures-oriented study for TAFE on 'Markets, products and delivery for the 21st century' (TAFE Queensland, 1997) global knowledge economy concluded that the 21st century labour market would be very different, it would require its workers to think like 'independent contractors' (Peters, 1991) rather than believe in the traditional employer-sponsored job security. Further, it saw an increasing need for Australians to be adaptable, life-long learners and for schools to assume responsibility for greater pre-service vocational education and training rather than the Technical And Further Education sectors, with the latter having a much more urgent role within the workforce and for adults returning to study.

Within a couple of years, the OECD developed a landmark paper recognising the impact of the global knowledge economy (*Learning Cities and Regions*, 1999:5) and emphasising the changes occurring in the Western world. Its observations were highly pertinent to the future role of schooling:

> OECD societies are rapidly becoming knowledge-based economies depending as never before on human resources. National and international economic resources are now defined in terms of knowledge and human skill capacities rather than the production of goods and output. Expanding people's skills and capacities is therefore fundamental to personal well being as well as the health of the wider economy as a whole. Learning skills and knowledge have now become the key factors in gaining national, regional and even urban economic advantage.

It is important to note the reference to 'personal well being', emphasising the intricate linking of living and working, the individual and the economy. For a long time in education, particularly secondary schooling, we have regarded the linking of schooling and working, or schooling and the economy, as not only of little importance but also rather unseemly.

Despite the growth of work experience programs and even vocational education programs, the association of school with business has been seen as an attack on liberal education. The well being of the individual, however, is essential to successful economies. At a big-picture political level, the Soviet Bloc where the individual was subjugated has gone. China's growth in recent years has been achieved by unleashing the capabilities of individuals. Personal 'wellness' includes music, literature, art, sport and all those things that we have traditionally associated with 'good' schooling, indeed, upbringing. However, today schools are concerned with the development of creativity, inventiveness and initiative in all young people, not just the few.

Despite this increasing recognition of global change, something continued to be wrong with Australian education. Under the weight of evidence that demanded a response from the education sector, it became increasingly apparent that something fundamental was missing. At the same time as research by the OECD was demonstrating the strong links between the level of education and unemployment, our school retention rates were declining from the strong days of the early 1990s where, following the Finn Review (1991) and the Carmichael Report (1992) dealing with post-compulsory education and training, school retention boomed. Increasing numbers of young people were facing an uncertain employment future.

At a personal level, this was confirmed during my employment with the Queensland government in 1999 and in the labour market area where direct links between low levels of schooling and long-term unemployment were obvious.

Increasingly, the labour market was looking for people who could value add using knowledge skills. The schooling sector, with notable exceptions, was not responding. It saw its main role as being traditional and academic, with vocational or applied studies for those who could not handle the academic. It failed to see the changes in the labour market that suggested all young Australians needed a very different schooling focus, one that converged both these learning areas, one that was in tune with their lives now and cognisant of the current and future working environment for young people.

At this time, I had the opportunity to establish a labour market research and policy unit for the Queensland State Government. Researchers from within this unit and from the University of Queensland explored a number of issues associated with employment and unemployment, including youth, ageing, ICT, capacity for learning, regional development and long-term unemployment. Much of the research started to direct attention to the findings of a European report:

> Tomorrow's society will be a society which invests in knowledge, a society of teaching and learning in which each individual will build up his or her own qualifications. In other words, a learning society.
>
> The European Commission, 1994:1

There is little evidence that Australia has applied this level of thinking to the implications for schooling based on the changes brought via the development of the global knowledge economy. We seem locked into political agendas about keeping up with the Joneses (that is, OECD countries), with traditional literacy, numeracy and the sciences, and then also keeping in tune with the 1950s by re-emphasising grades and rankings in class!

The paucity of strategic vision for schooling, which focused instead on funding and the attempt to drag schooling to a lowest common denominator, was roundly rejected by the Australian public. If anything, it reflected the desire of many Australians to aspire to the best possible education for their children.

Our nation is yet to break out of a mindset about what the best possible education should mean for our young people. In many ways Australia still has not focused, from a policy direction, on the massive changes occurring in the labour market, including the demise of old jobs and the continual creation of new, largely knowledge-based ones. We worry about the short-term issue of unemployment rather than the long-term future of our human capital. We recognise skill shortages, but have not actually seen how these skills have become different and more challenging and complex because of the knowledge era.

While a number of educators, myself included, disagree with some of the directions taken in the United Kingdom, such as the School League Tables whose ratings are based on dubious educational outcomes, at least there is evidence that they are initiating macro-schooling change to meet the labour market demands of a global knowledge economy.

One could say that the business of the education system is to manage the different learning opportunities and achievements required by individuals and society for the future.

Barker, 1998/99

There are certainly corporations in Australia doing their own research into how best to deal with the new knowledge economy. A forward-thinking state general manager at Unisys commissioned a grant to research the relationship between IT, employment and regional Australia. The question posed for the study was, 'Does Queensland and its regions have the labour force to enable strong participation in the knowledge economy?' The study suggested:

The new global knowledge economy is rewarding those societies that have [transformed] and are transforming their labour forces from the traditional industrial paradigm to a knowledge era paradigm. In the emerging labour force, a key focus is on employability of people for both the new and modified jobs, that is, those jobs created or modified through the digital and knowledge revolution. Part of the transformation of the labour force is in the destruction or at least severe modification to traditional lower skilled jobs and conversely the creation of new jobs requiring different and generally more complex skill sets. The old jobs that have gone will not come back and the new jobs are subject to continuous change. This requires adaptability and life-long learning in the workforce. Caught in this collision between the traditional industrial economy and the knowledge economy are the people whose job expectations and skills do not fit.

DEET, 1999: 21

As information and communication technology is enabling this new era, it has profound implications for schooling, way beyond thinking that schools simply have to teach IT literacy. Lipnack and Stamps (1997) argued that 'the onrushing explosion in information and communication technologies makes change in how we learn inevitable'. That was seven years ago and we know just how much change has happened in this period, but schools still remain very much the same.

The power shift

All good parenting is directed towards giving the child an ever-increasing set of competencies that gradually enable the child to act more and more on his or her own. Good parenting is essentially about 'letting go', in the confidence that the skills learned in the past will be more effective in dealing with novelty, than would prescription. The same weaning principle has to be applied to the child's intellectual development. Schools, and parents, have therefore to start a dynamic process through which young people are progressively weaned from their dependence on teachers and institutions and given the confidence to manage their own learning, collaborating with colleagues as appropriate, and using a range of resources and learning situations.

Education 2000 Trust, 1997

Professor Beare's Angelica would argue, at the age of five, that she is starting school without the need for dependence on teachers, but with a desire to have teachers work with her to explore her world. She also does not want them controlling her or her search for her world view, but our society's litigious nature and concern for the custodial role of the school means that teachers have to worry as much about the 'duty of care' as about teaching and learning.

The British position is a good starting point. However, it is less about weaning the child and more about weaning teachers and parents from their dependence on managing and controlling young people through traditional curriculum, classroom management and assessment. If we needed a transition point though, the British position is one that needs to be considered as part of helping schools and teachers become part of the new world.

As Gary Marx (2003) describes:

We are going to have increasing numbers of students coming to our schools with more information on a lot of topics than their teachers have. It's already happening. They may have had more time than the teachers did last night to mine the Internet, which means that teachers will be using their higher-level skills and probably enjoying teaching even more. It means we have a lot of kids with not much life experience who have a lot of data and information. The teacher will help move those kids from raw data and information towards usable knowledge and then, we hope, towards wisdom. Teachers will not only be subject matter specialists, but they will also be facilitators of learning, orchestrators of learning, partners with those students in learning. They won't be upset at all if a child comes to school and has more information on a topic than the teacher, because they are partners in learning. They almost teach each other.

Many young people, certainly by secondary school, have ICT skills far superior to many of their teachers. Their skills directly connect young people to the knowledge world and to learning. They are surfing the Internet, networking, collaborating, accessing vast levels of information and taking risks, exploring and manipulating information technology. These skills can no longer be overlooked, but must be incorporated into a 'working together' school environment.

As educators, we can learn from this technology designed so effectively to engage the attention of young children. We have to face the fact that the Internet has revolutionised the balance between the power of the adult and the status of children (Aphek, 2001). There has been a power shift in who holds the information and who does not. The implications for a knowledge era school lie in how this power shift manifests itself, and in the learning environment, in teachers relinquishing the need to control. Professor Elliot Eisner, Stanford University, Art and Education, and one of the great curriculum gurus, concluded his article, 'Preparing for today and tomorrow' (*Educational Leadership*, December 2003/January 2004), by arguing:

> Preparation for tomorrow is best served by meaningful education today ... we will realise that genuine reform of our schools requires a shift in paradigms from those with which we have become comfortable to others that more adequately address the potential that humans have for shaping not only the world, but themselves.

This insightful comment is highly pertinent to the transformation process as it addresses exactly the challenge for teachers. Sophie, a Year 8 student, reflects the expectation on teachers from the student perspective:

> At some schools they [teachers] have forgotten what their job is. They keep making rules thinking they will make their school and their students perfect but it doesn't work that way at all ... Not only is a controlled school harder for the teacher, it also stifles student learning. No one likes it or benefits.

Young people and trust

The industrial era school fails to recognise the skills of young people and introduces them to learning and a culture that is out of step with their world. There is an important element of trust involved—trust that young people are willing to work with us and not dismiss us. Allee (1997: 212) suggests:

> The key elements of a knowledge culture are a climate of trust and openness in an environment where constant learning and experimentation are highly valued, appreciated and supported.

To what extent do we have schools that are premised on trust and openness? Trusting our young people, for example, as they lead us in often very non-traditional school ways, into some experimental and exciting directions with IT would be a mark of a knowledge era school.

But what are the consequences of not engaging in a mutually trusting relationship? Allowing for a percentage of schools dealing with larger social issues beyond their control, media reports indicate increased levels of student violence in schools. Some people would suggest that trust is not something we will be able to share and, in fact, schools will have to increase their focus on discipline to manage these apparently unruly young people. Reports direct attention to 13- to 14-year-old boys who 'were most likely to have broken the rules. Overall boys accounted for 80 per cent of the expulsions and 77 per cent of the suspensions' (*The Times*, 31 July 2004). Of course this will be the case, and soon we will have greater numbers of girls, or rather, young women added to the statistic. These issues should help us understand and respond to the question of why schools need to change and why we should start to see problems in schools as created by the traditional culture of schooling rather than young people.

In Australia, we have increased school retention remarkably over the last 20 years, not because schooling has become better but because in the emerging knowledge era there are fewer permanent and full-time jobs in the traditional lower-skilled areas of the labour market. This in itself has become a problem for all young people. They have to stay on and be subjected largely to curricula designed for the smaller numbers of previous years that stayed at school to go on to university. Even today, with large shortages in traditional skills, people still look for academic results from school at the end of Year 12.

This is not the problem of young people. It is the problem of society, governments and educators. We have not created appropriate curricula and learning environments and have kept schooling out of touch with a transformed world.

IQ and EQ: The softer skills

Two other important issues are IQ (intelligence quotient) and EQ (emotional quotient). A really important question we will have to confront is whether it is still appropriate to equate intelligence with familiar subject disciplines (Maths, Geography, Chemistry, History and so on) and academic success.

Canadian intellectual John Ralston Saul suggests:

> ... every society [era] has its own definition of intelligence, and then puts forward a mythology, an education system, which gives comfort to that idea of intelligence. The practical result is that different parts of society rise to the surface ... What we have now defined as intelligence is very, very narrow.

> (a discussion related in Ellis, *Goodbye Babylon*, 2002: 215)

One of the hardest things for us to think about as adults is this issue of IQ, associated only with academic intelligence. Our industrial world defines it not only narrowly, but also so that a majority of the population cannot be considered as, or be successful at, being intelligent. There has been an intended schooling process that enabled those who were 'more intelligent' in industrial era academic terms to continue and finish school and then go on to university while those who were 'less intelligent', were destined to leave and fill trade, semi-skilled and unskilled jobs. As we have discussed, these jobs have diminished in number or disappeared and greater training and skill is needed for the new jobs being created. Many of these jobs have little to do with traditional subject-defined intelligence.

For so many young people, schooling's traditional subject base and recognition of a narrowly defined intelligence mean that their schooling is largely irrelevant. Of course, people will say there is more to school than subjects, but it is this traditional subject base that helps keep schooling industrial in nature even though over the past few decades we have added new subject disciplines such as Information Technology, Business Management, Hospitality and Tourism. Proponents of these subjects have had to fight the traditionalists for them to be recognised as 'academic' and many schools still do not give them the status of 'real' subjects. Physics is still more important than Multimedia.

Schooling has to confront the issue of IQ and start to recognise that intelligence today needs to be defined differently. If more young people are coming to school with high motivation and well-defined skills of learning, exploring, discovering and collaborating, we need to look at how schooling can enhance these and take young people further, rather than trying to fit them into the industrial IQ box. My comments are not to refute the essential enabling skills associated with literacy, incorporating numeracy and technology, but rather to reject the primacy given, particularly in secondary schooling, to subjects as opposed to learning.

Where does emotional intelligence (referred to as EQ) fit in? Emotional intelligence means how we, as people, learn to manage ourselves, our relationships and our interactions with our environment. We use EQ to make decisions, to problem solve, to reflect and to organise our relationships and ourselves. It is one area that has been overlooked in schooling. It has been part of the 'hidden curriculum'; something that occurs by chance and often develops quite poorly. Schools do say that they are concerned for the cognitive, social, physical, emotional and spiritual being, but when we actually look at what we do, most attention is given to the cognitive. There are very few real applied learning experiences that schools have incorporated into their curriculum to teach EQ.

The complexities of the modern world demand that we bring together or converge teaching for EQ as much as for IQ.

Daniel Goleman, in his article 'What makes a leader?' (*Harvard Business Review*, January 2004) describes five components of EQ. He directs our attention to critical components of learning that are not formally embedded in school curricula:

What makes a leader?	Definition	Hallmarks
Self-awareness	Ability to recognise and understand your moods, emotions and drives as well as their effects on others Ability to control or redirect disruptive impulses and moods	¬ Self-confidence ¬ Realistic self-assessment ¬ Self-deprecating sense of humour
Self-regulation	Ability to control or redirect disruptive impulses and moods Ability to think before acting	¬ Trustworthiness and integrity ¬ Comfort with ambiguity ¬ Openness to change

What makes a leader?	Definition	Hallmarks
Motivation	A passion to work for reasons that go beyond status, (achievement) or money A propensity to pursue goals with energy and persistence	¬ Strong drive to achieve ¬ Optimism, even in the face of failure
Empathy	Ability to understand the emotional make-up of other people Skill in treating people according to their emotional reactions	¬ Cross-cultural sensitivity ¬ Service to others ¬ Understanding in working with other people and capacity to build up other people
Social skill	Proficiency in managing relationships and building networks An ability to find common ground and build rapport	¬ Persuasiveness ¬ Leading change ¬ Team builder and leader

You can see why emotional intelligence is a difficult area to teach and hard for young people to learn. Many schools and education policy makers would argue that these things *are* taught in schools. Currently, however, they are accidental or incidental to the formal subject curriculum. They cannot be assessed in traditional ways. (Imagine how the final Year 12 exams would cope with them!) Schools, teachers and possibly parents may always regard EQ components as less important, while the familiar and traditional industrial era academic outcomes are seen as the mark of success. However, without the attributes of EQ, young people will increasingly find it difficult to manage their lives in this complex and rapidly changing job market.

New City School, St Louis, USA

Under Dr Tom Hoerr's leadership, the school has been implementing the theory of Multiple Intelligences since 1988, developing models for alternative forms of student assessment, and gaining national recognition for its work. Over 50 000 copies of two books written by Tom and the teachers of the school about their work with MI has been sold, the school has hosted four MI conferences, and 500–700 educators visit the school each year. (In December 2005 New City's new MI Library will be opened by Howard Gardner.) Tom facilitates the ASCD MI Network and gives presentations on MI and leadership throughout the USA and around the world. The importance of the personal intelligences (PI) is stressed in his talks.

According to Tom, skills in the personal intelligences—both interpersonal and intrapersonal under Gardner's MI model (Goldman's Emotional Intelligence, EQ)—are what lead to success in school.

Tom believes that although there are many things about New City which set it apart from other schools, one of the most important is its focus on Personal Intelligence (PI). A common phrase used by him is 'who you are is more important than what you know'. The school places such value on the personal intelligences that it devotes the first page of each student's report, called 'Page One', to them.

Tom writes, 'Of course, we absolutely need to challenge students academically, but that's just the beginning. To truly position our students for success, we need to help them grow in areas such as confidence, motivation, responsibility, teamwork, and so on. We accomplish this in many different ways. For us, that means a lot of discussing incidents with kids, in lieu of just throwing out punishments. We have a major emphasis on having kids reflect on their actions and discuss other alternatives.'

All students at New City have the same five rules to live by (which are posted in all classrooms and above the exit form all buildings): Truth; Trust; No Putdowns; Personal Best; Active Listening.

<http://www.newcityschool.org>

If all schools really focused on teaching for emotional intelligence, recognising personal intelligences and creating the school cultures to support them, we would find fewer reports on school violence and ill-discipline. Boys of 13 to 14 years of age might in fact be enjoying school, engaged in it and succeeding.

The imperative for a new education paradigm

Starting about five years ago, some of Australia's leading education academics identified the critical need for secondary schools to recognise the working world as it would be 20 years from now and made recommendations as to how schools could adjust their teaching methods accordingly.

The 2002 article 'The future school: seven radical differences' written by Professor Hedley Beare can be regarded as seminal. Corroborative research by other well-known education academics (Hargreaves, 2004; Caldwell, 2004, 2005; Miller and Bentley, 2004) about the future of schooling has been documented in similar terms.

Currently, the vast majority of schools in Australia are still basing their teaching assumptions on the world as it was 30 to 40 years ago—that is, while teachers themselves might be more child-centred, leading to fewer cases of corporal punishment or punitive teacher behaviour, the paradigm in which they teach remains unchanged. Lord David Puttnam, English writer, director and producer, tells a story that suggests we may still teach as if we were living 100 years ago:

There's a story I try and tell teachers and I think it's worth repeating. If you time-travelled a very good doctor from the year 1900 to the year 2000 into an operating theatre, he literally would be an exercise in incompetence. He could make a cup of tea, take the patient's pulse and do nothing else at all, because basically, technology has obviated his original skills. You take a schoolteacher from 1900, put her in a classroom in the year 2000, give her some chalk and a blackboard, she in most subjects could teach a class.

As a pre-emptive action, Australia has the opportunity to enhance its competitive position in the global knowledge economy. Through the pioneering efforts of some educators, and thanks to the parents who understand the rationale and have supported the changes, Australia has the benefit of experiencing first-hand how the knowledge era school functions.

There is now an imperative for knowledge era schooling. The globalised marketplace, the transforming youth labour market, and the ubiquitous development of information and communication technologies are major reasons why schooling should review the way it prepares young Australians for the future. By world standards, it is prudent that Australia continues pushing its schools in order to help young people develop their capabilities and their world views to thrive in this developing environment.

The need for constant improvement is the same for schools Australia-wide, whether public, Catholic or independent, because for the first time, a national perspective has given way to an international one. Indeed, educators worldwide, in developed and developing economies, can see the nature of work changing and are hungry to adopt best practice in schooling.

Best practice schooling creates opportunities for individuals based on their natural strengths and aptitudes. It has a culture that accepts and works with young people so that their skills are acknowledged and they have the disposition and skill to deal with the world as it is. Schools need to take on board the key principles as outlined by education academics such as Hedley Beare (2001; 2002), Brian Caldwell (2004; 2005) and David Hargreaves (2004a and 2004b). From these principles we can develop the framework for establishing appropriate models for knowledge era schooling across the educational spectrum.

Command-and-control is simply unsuited to the complex, unpredictable demands of organisational life in the knowledge age.

Bentley, 2002

Of course, not everyone will agree with the rationale for change set out in this chapter. Neil Postman (in Aphek, 2001) suggests that today's children have lost their childhood to media and technology that is ultimately 'dumbing down' both children and adults. Postman believes we should be slowly releasing the adult-controlled world to young people. In fact, this is how it has always been, but the world that young people are part of does not allow a slow release unless we cocoon and continue to overprotect young people. Postman's position is really quite untenable in the knowledge era unless we are prepared to wind back the clock and reduce or block access by young people to television, multimedia, marketing, the Internet, mobile phones and so on.

While, as a parent, this might seem attractive, I also know that it cannot be done. In previous generations it was possible to prolong childhood because parents were the centre of young people's lives and, with assistance from schools, we actually controlled the lives of young people much more. It was easier because their access to information and also to communication tools was limited. Now they come to school with attitudes born of the immediacy of their access to the world at large and as a result have a greater freedom of mind.

Such cognitive freedom equates to greater physical and verbal freedom. These young people have developed attitudes that do not sit well with middle-aged, subject-trained teachers and rules-bound school management staff who believe that this is what parents expect of them. The reality is that many parents, fearful of the new world that their children are generally revelling in, expect their schools to provide control and discipline alongside a strong liberal, academic education. Many parents still look for this in schooling, even when they know from their own life–work experiences that much of this is irrelevant to the real world of the 21st century.

Don Tapscott (in Aphek, 2001) describes another view. He sees children of the Internet as being different from Postman's child. The Internet child is active, engaged and creative. Children of the Internet era learn differently and explore things that are beyond the adult-managed curriculum. They are much more in control of their own learning. When we put this into a Western context, we recognise that over 70 per cent of American young people use the Internet and over 70 per cent of Australian young people are Internet users (ABS, 2004). China has 70 000 000 home Internet users and most middle and senior school students have used it. They are living in the new world of connectivity, speed and the growth of intangible value.

BLUR: THE SPEED OF CHANGE IN A CONNECTED ECONOMY
An economy is the way people use resources to fulfil their desires. The specific ways they do this have changed several times through history and are shifting yet again—this time driven by three forces—**connectivity, speed and the growth of intangible value**. Because we are so caught up in the whirlwind of this transition we are experiencing it as a blur.

Davis and Meyer, 1999

This has been happening in our world for the past decade and it is the world of young people now. Why is it taking us so long to understand this reality and change our schools?

Modelling for the future

We like to be consulted on problems that concern us rather than decisions being made for us. We also don't want to be treated like kids anymore; we want to be treated with a degree of trust. We'd like to be disciplined like adults and stop having disruptions during classes. We expect that students in Year 10 are ready and willing to learn and that they will be mature and responsible about their schooling.

Leah (Year 9)

Where does change begin? If Australia and its young people are going to take up the opportunities of this new world and become contributors, then it only makes common sense that the schooling sector, particularly that traditionally called the secondary sector, needs to take on this responsibility to change. Schools need to become leaders of change.

In many ways, beginning the process of transformation is extremely hard. Many schools and their staff, even when attuned to the changes brought with the advent of the global knowledge economy, can feel that change in such a fundamental way is too risky in its potential effect on university entrance results.

It is the schools and their principals and teachers that recognise the changed youth labour market—both nationally and globally—and the need for a more widely educated and skilled school graduate that will represent the next wave of major educational reformists in this country. But they need a model, a working example of a secondary school that has made the transformation and has proven it can be done without any drop in familiar schooling outcomes, like university entrance rates.

A review of the National Quality Schooling Framework (NQSF) whose charter is to 'implement innovative and evidence-based projects to improve student learning outcomes in your school' shows evidence that a number of schools have embarked on the road to transformation.

Schools on the road to transformation

Kingscliffe High School, NSW put in place programs to ensure that all students and staff have well-developed ICT skills and has encouraged teachers to integrate ICT across all curriculum areas.

Penrhos Junior School, Western Australia has initiated a program of observing, developing, and sharing 'best practice' amongst its teachers and has used NQSF resources and ideas that have helped teachers to be better connected in terms of their thinking and approach to the classroom.

Box Hill Senior Secondary School, Victoria, a Year 10 to 12 school, has taken significant steps towards a transformed school environment, including an empowered student body who are consulted and contribute to school decision-making, and a large commitment to IT including a campus-wide wireless network allowing classes and study to continue anywhere in the school.

It is true to say there are many examples of schools taking the initiative to maintain their relevance and effectiveness in engaging young people. It is also true to say that only some schools are at the point of real transformation, let alone a school that has transformed itself for the knowledge era.

Before we move on to in-depth case study explorations, we need to think carefully about the criteria necessary for transformation in the schools that are educating our young people. In Chapter 4, a clear set of guiding principles to transforming a school for the knowledge era is defined and discussed. These principles for change are dynamic and as our experience of a transformed schooling environment grows, so too does our thinking.

4 | Criteria for knowledge era schooling

> Learning and teaching should not stand on opposite
> banks and just watch the river flow by; instead, they
> should embark together on a journey down the water.
> Through an active, reciprocal exchange, teaching can
> strengthen learning how to learn.
>
> Edwards, Gandini and Forman, 1998

A clash of paradigms

Today's world is not simply a clash of cultures (generations X and Y versus the baby boomers), or the difference between maturity and immaturity, or between knowledge and lack of knowledge; it is a massive clash of paradigms: the knowledge era versus the industrial era. Schooling, its managers and teachers, are largely locked into the control and directed culture of the industrial era: management control, knowledge and curriculum control, behaviour control and the worst of all, assessment and credentialing control. It is no wonder that the media, internationally, presents stories about increasing discipline problems in schools.

The clash of paradigms is shown in the following table.

Knowledge era schooling	Industrial era schooling
Attitude of sharing authority	Teacher control attitude
¬ teachers and young people work together to create knowledge	¬ teachers pass on knowledge
¬ people empowered	¬ power concentrated

Knowledge era schooling	Industrial era schooling

Freedom to explore and take risks
¬ young people have space and
  time to learn
	Controlled environment where teachers
	manage learning
	¬ inflexible time and space in closed
	  classrooms

A culture of change ¬ develops resiliency ¬ develops independence ¬ develops adaptability ¬ develops creativity and innovation ¬ is entrepreneurial ¬ is part of the real world	Highly structured and change averse ¬ fosters only limited coping skills; inflexible ¬ fosters compliance and rigidity ¬ fosters only managed innovation ¬ is supervisory ¬ is uniform and conformist ¬ is divorced from the real world

Models the 21st century
¬ teaches to manage life–work
¬ develops multiple intelligences
¬ develops EQ and IQ
¬ converges the curriculum
  (academic and vocational)
¬ focuses on student learning
¬ encourages self-management
¬ is customised to the individual
	Models the 19th and 20th centuries
	¬ teaches subjects towards traditional
	  careers
	¬ focuses on intelligence quotient
	¬ focuses on academic intelligence/IQ
	¬ has subject/academic curriculum
	¬ focuses on subject learning
	¬ manages students
	¬ assumes 'one size fits all'

Learning
¬ encourages culture of change
  and innovation
¬ fosters creativity
¬ self-managing and self-directed learning
	Instructing
	¬ is controlled, uniform and consistent
	¬ fosters compliance
	¬ adult-directed learning and
	  management

This table shows a tangible difference between the two worlds of schooling and why we have a clash of paradigms. Knowledge era schooling suggests that change cannot be traditional, slow and incremental. Young people now demand that we as educators and parents transform their learning experiences.

We know that every generation of adolescents has been criticised for its intolerance of authority, its selfishness and its 'unsocial' behaviours. However, we also know today that this generation (generation Y) is very different even from recent previous generations or sub-generations. We know that over the past five years, young people have been exposed to and have had to deal with much more information than any previous generation. Older generations can put change into some historical perspective, but most young people are immersed in continual change and this creates a range of emotions and behaviours. Our job is to help them understand their world and develop their own world views. This will help prepare young people for the uncertain future. However, it is also hard for us because we tend not to understand the ramifications of rapid change very well either. I do know that to try to make sense of the world in traditional terms will leave a huge gap between us and current and future generations.

We all need to learn to operate bi-culturally and teach our students to operate the same way. The basic message to young people needs to be: 'Hey kid, this is an environment in which we give each other respect, but we recognise that the world you will need to deal with may be different from ours. In your group you can act the way your culture accepts, but in our shared culture these are the expectations that we both must follow so that we can function happily together. We too need to learn to operate more effectively in working with your world. There are strengths that we both bring to this collaboration in learning, and we both accept that exactly the same values and standards should apply to each other.'

The fundamental concept of bi-culturalism in schools is that we need to be able to understand, operate with, respect and help young people learn and succeed from their world-view point. At the same time, we as educators need to be able to help them to effectively understand our world and expectations and to learn to live with them, but not embrace them. We have to be able to create this understanding so that we can cohabit and collaborate rather than travel completely separate paths and become embroiled in conflict. However, we have to use processes that are in tune with their expectations about how we might achieve this. It is not a process of authority and control, but rather of working together.

Where does learning theory fit in?

Learning theorists have focused on the concept of working together in the early years of schooling, and from them comes considerable sense in relation to the learning culture of the knowledge era school.

While Piaget may have emphasised the role of peer conflict in promoting learning, there is more to be gained from creating a context of collaboration where young people and older people work together through learning. Berk and Winsler (1995: 19–20) argue that:

> ... the Vygotskian perspective suggests that what is important is not so much who participates in social exchanges—adult–child or child–child—as how partners organise their joint activity. Conflict and disagreement do not seem to be as important in fostering development as the extent to which differences of opinion are resolved, responsibility shared between participants, and discourse, cooperation and mutual respect.

Vygotsky (in Berk and Winsler, 1995) reasoned that when young students work alone they focus solely on the goal of their activity (for example, do a puzzle, build a tower) and rarely stop to think about their thinking. When they work in partnership with an adult, the adult can help to break the task down into its different parts, can suggest different avenues that the young person might try, support the young person in suggestions and attempts, and reflect with them on the success of their efforts. The young person is then working in their Zone of Proximal Development (ZPD), which is the zone between what young people can learn independently and what they can learn in collaboration with a teacher. They not only master the skill of the new task but also they move to a higher level of cognitive development where they have begun to think about their own thinking.

Vygotsky's theory is a sociocultural one. He asserts that learning leads to development. As the young person works with an adult or more expert partner within their ZPD, learning plays a significant role in leading their development forward.

The implication for younger students may be that the learning program becomes neither young person centred nor teacher directed but originated by the young person and framed by the teacher. This way the adult can structure the learning environment so that the student is working in their ZPD. There is a continual reciprocal relationship between the teacher and student, between what the student knows already and where the learning will go.

The implication for older students in both primary and secondary schools is an extension of this. It emphasises the importance of the teaching–learning relationship and how teachers structure learning experiences, increasingly applying greater freedom and avenues for risk-taking as young people develop skills for learning.

I am applying this theory across schooling and rejecting the more traditional one that suggests learning at older stages is different. Early learning theories are based very closely on working together and collaborating and then building a culture of teaching for independent operation. Recognising that young people will arrive at this point at different stages, a framework that allows increasing independence to be built into the older person–younger person relationship through the schooling journey is essential.

The development of the skill of learning—more specifically the skill for self-directed or life-long learning—can be effectively seen in the context of scaffolding. The term is an old one, but more frequently is used today to help describe learning within the context of new curriculum opportunities, such as the Victorian Essential Learning Standards (<http://vels.vcaa.vic.edu.au/>), Tasmania's Essential Learnings for All (<http://www.doe.tased.edu.au>) or the more assessment-oriented Queensland Curriculum, Assessment and Reporting (<http://education.qld.gov.au/qcar>) that puts learning into the context of a relational activity through the whole of compulsory schooling.

Scaffolding

The child is viewed as a building, actively constructing him or her self. The social environment is the necessary support system that allows the child to move forward and continue to build new competencies.

Berk and Winsler, 1995: 26

Scaffolding or building construction sees engagement through collaborative problem solving, developing shared understanding, working towards common goals, negotiation and compromise, warm relationships and developing self-regulation and learning (Berk and Winsler, 1995: 26–101). Berk and Winsler further develop the work of Wood and his collaborators on scaffolding and use Zygotsky's Zone of Proximate Development. They say (p. 29) that learning involves 'structuring the task and the surrounding environment so that the demands on the child at any given time are at an appropriately challenging level, and constantly adjusting the amount of adult intervention to the child's current needs and abilities'. The context of this is building towards the teacher (adult) 'relinquishing control and assistance as soon as the child can work independently' (p. 30).

Knowledge era schooling also should be seen, therefore, within a context of learning from early learning. Malaguzzi, who established the Reggio Emelia approach, says: 'Stand aside for a while and leave the room for learning, observe carefully what children do, and then, if you have understood well, perhaps teaching will be different from before' (Edwards, Gandini and Forman, 1998: 82). This is 'active education' where older and younger people collaborate in the process. Edwards et al. (p. 83) say:

> Learning and teaching should not stand on opposite banks and just watch the river flow by; instead, they should embark together on a journey down the water. Through an active, reciprocal exchange, teaching can strengthen learning how to learn.

If we consider briefly these learning theorists within the context of the 21st century knowledge era we will begin to think about the notion of a schooling culture that customises learning through the collaboration of educators and young people from the early years throughout their schooling. Today we must move beyond the behaviourism that characterises so much of our schooling. We need to move to schooling that concentrates on the dynamics of younger and older people in interaction at a personal, individual level and where schooling scaffolds learning for the individual.

Criteria for knowledge era schooling

Let us now look at the key criteria that can be used by schools to develop into this model, and help move our young people and our nation forward into our very own new world.

Creating a knowledge era transformation in a schooling environment is difficult. It means having the courage as a principal to consider what constitutes knowledge era schooling and the courage as a teacher to implement a new approach. For us to seriously consider what schooling is relevant to young people in the 21st century, we need to define the criteria by which we as parents and educators can identify knowledge era schools or schools that have made a commitment to transformation.

Schooling must respond to the world of the 21st century. It is the world and future of young people. We must work with them to help them develop their own world view (Beare, 2001) and to develop their talents and dispositions to be able to work with and lead change. To move into the knowledge era and escape from the industrial era, schools need to closely consider the following change issues:

First, there must be a commitment from the leadership and staff of a school to completely refocus from an environment that values adult knowledge and authority to one that shares knowledge creation and authority with young people.

Second, schools need to provide the culture that allows young people to take risks: to have space, time and the freedom to explore. Freedom is a key environmental feature of the knowledge era school and a difficult one to manage, not only in relation to issues such as levels of maturity, authority and safety, but also because we live in an increasingly litigious society and managers and teachers are tempted to be over-cautious.

Third, schools need to develop a culture of change. Change needs to be central to all that young people experience in school because through it young people will develop resiliency, adaptability and personal flexibility to become not only people who can cope with change but also agents of it.

Fourth, schools should be able to model the world in which young people live and in which they will work and better customise the relationship through learning. There needs to be a life–work focus and an environment enabled by information and communication technology, that is, one in touch with a global society. We should revisit what knowledge means in a schooling context and acknowledge that intelligence goes beyond the academic and includes multiple intelligences and individual talents that can operate in a social, collaborative sense. This means converging academic and vocational and creating active learning.

Fifth, a focus on knowledge era teaching and learning skills that includes:
¬ collaboration and teaming
¬ sharing leadership
¬ negotiating to arrive at shared expectations
¬ engagement management (managing learning rather than classrooms)
¬ creating and managing knowledge
¬ self-management
¬ the disposition and skill for self-directed learning.

This new era does not only reflect on secondary schooling but also the totality of the schooling experience. While secondary schools are the key, in the short term, to bridging the gap between the industrial society and the knowledge society, the knowledge era needs to be reflected across learning from the very early years. It will be in the early and junior years that we can most disadvantage young people. Indeed, we can turn them away from school learning because they are the children of the knowledge era. They are not simply experiencing, as are older people, a transformation that can be articulated as 'what is happening' but rather this world is all they know. They live it and if we continue to foster industrial values and learning methodologies they will not benefit from schooling. The next few chapters will reflect on changing developmental stages and how people learn. The focus will be on exploring the five criteria for knowledge era schooling:

1   An attitude of sharing authority
2   Freedom to explore and take risks
3   A culture of change
4   Modelling the 21st century
5   Different learning and teaching skills: self-management and self-directed learning.

Sharing authority | 5

Imagine our kids at 35, having left home five years
earlier, with limited job prospects, who can't afford their own
homes or even to start families, faced with an
ageing population to support and watching wealth being
generated overseas because that is where the
innovative, entrepreneurial knowledge work and workers have
gone. If this continues and we do not commit
to major transformation then we will find that the creative,
wealth-generating work will occur in countries such as
Hong Kong and not Australia.

Knowledge era schooling criterion 1:
An attitude of sharing authority

There must be a commitment from the leadership and staff of a school to
completely refocus from an environment that values adult knowledge and
authority to one that shares knowledge creation and authority with young
people.

The comfort of tradition

A lucky few might say that their school days were the happiest days of their lives, but we would all say that school was adult-dominated and learning was teacher-directed, that there were detentions, and that teachers knew more than we did. The principal was in control and teachers had authority because they were both adults and teachers, as well as possessing knowledge that we needed.

The school we went to was familiar, based on generations of education tradition. Today, as parents, we check whether these same familiar attitudes and behaviours exist in the school to which our children go. We look for values, often associated with religion. Although fewer of us attend church today, we believe that we want schools to teach the church's values and perhaps offer religious education of some kind. We look for security and safety, and at how ably the school cares for our children. We want our children to be protected. Generally, we seek good uniform dress standards and a well-disciplined environment. We associate discipline with values, uniform with standards and both with the development of character. Uniform is discipline, discipline is image and we associate that with pride. We expect traditional core subjects to dominate the timetable with adequate time also being given to the elective subjects. Our major concern is that Maths and English are emphasised and that the 'less important' subjects do not distract our children.

This is the prototype of an industrial era school. It does not matter much whether it is a high fee, well-established and selective school or a public school in a low socioeconomic area, each will have a very similar attitude to learning. The schools' academic results may differ markedly, they may have contrasting class sizes, they will offer very different co-curricular and elective programs and their teachers may be paid differently, but they will still have the same attitude towards young people and their learning.

Teachers will see young people as children needing to be taught subjects and skills just as they were taught subjects and skills. They will see young people as needing to be managed and controlled, just as they were managed and controlled. They will see boys as having more behaviour issues and presenting greater discipline problems. They will want to give more attention to those they believe will be successful academically and go to university. They will generally have a negative regard for vocational courses except as a means for removing more difficult students from mainstream subjects. This is well illustrated in Melbourne or London, for example, where the media sets out to rank schools on one criterion: external examination results and university entrance scores. Some schools limit their Year 12 class sizes to 15 students so that the students can be better coached for exam results, regardless of how many graduates from the previous year remain at university.

These schools are operating within a culture designed to fit the needs of the industrial era. The United Kingdom mirrors some of Australia's attitudes. In his autobiography, Harrow teacher and first-grade soccer referee David Elleray said:

Teachers should not set out to be liked. The easiest word is yes but the important word is no ... They [teaching and refereeing] are both about discipline and control ... I believe that firmness creates the right environment ...

How unfortunate that such people do not have the capacity to see that today's world demands young people who will engage in the joy of learning and that developing a love of schooling will produce far more positive outcomes for the individual and for society.

Fundamentally, industrial era schools do not have the culture to develop creative, innovative and entrepreneurial young people as a major outcome of their schooling or indeed as being central to their learning processes. This is not to say that such young people cannot be found in these schools or do not graduate from them. Despite their schooling rather than as a result of it, small numbers of students have often been innovative. However, most school graduates do not see themselves as innovative and entrepreneurial. The 20 to 30 per cent who leave school before finishing Year 12 often see themselves as failures. It is hard for such young people to believe in themselves or in the society in which they live. They certainly will not pass on to their children anything positive about schooling.

Society still believes too strongly in the theory of 'established models', that is, that schooling can only operate successfully when its operations are based on established models of school practice. In simple terms: 'If it does not look and feel like the schools of our youth, there must be something wrong.'

Schools shape our future

Another concern about industrial schooling relates to Australia's future competitiveness. The knowledge era and its global knowledge economy require many, rather than just a few, young people to be knowledge workers, innovative and self-directed life-long learners. Employers seek:

- independent, creative and critical thinkers
- people with problem-solving abilities
- great communicators, with clients and colleagues.

AC Nielson Research, 1999

Networking in schooling is becoming an increasingly important part of the school landscape in relation to creating the freedom of opportunities for young people. Ringwood Secondary College in Victoria has developed industry networks to increase the opportunity for young people to develop the knowledge and skills needed in today's workplace. Goondiwindi State High School in Queensland has developed networks with employers to ensure that disengaged young people obtain the motivation to develop their learning skills and school outcomes. In both, there is the recognition that schools are pivotal in preparing students for workplace realities.

Developing learning skills

Ringwood Secondary College in Melbourne has recognised that one way in which these skills are developed is through close networking with industry. Young people, in contact with employers from local business and industry, are able to understand the workplace and how these skills are applied. Using federal government funding to address skill shortfalls in the automotive, engineering and manufacturing sectors and in consultation with major industry leaders and TAFE, Ringwood Secondary College established an Automotive and Manufacturing Technology Centre (AMTC).

Phillips, 2005

We cannot simply leave the development of the skills demanded by employers to universities and TAFEs. Not only do they not teach these skills, but also years are needed—particularly at a formative age—for these attributes to be developed and enhanced. Innovation, independence, and the disposition to learn cannot simply be add-ons that young people get sometime in their post-school lives. In fact, most young people start kindergarten and school with at least the first two of the aforementioned skills. Over 13 years, many schools unwittingly do their best to repress these skills. Goondiwindi State High, like Ringwood Secondary College, is doing its best to extend these skills through networking with its community and employers.

Goondiwindi State High School, Queensland

Goondiwindi State High School, in a rural community about 375 kilometres south-west of Brisbane, increased its Year 12 completion rate from 54 per cent in 1999 to 89 per cent in 2000.

This remarkable result was achieved through a partnership between the Department of Employment and Training, the school, local rural industry and the wider community. Year 11 students were provided training opportunities by 96 employers, and school-based traineeships were offered in 17 industry areas. Participating students were required to complete only four school subjects, as well as the requirements of their training plan.

In order to build upon this achievement, a partnership between the Department of Employment and Training, Education Queensland, local rural industry and the community has been formed to establish a Goondiwindi Rural Technology Skills Centre.

For further information, including details on the target group and responsible agency, follow the link to Initiatives targeting Recommendation 20 at:
<http://www.mceetya.edu.au/stepping/casestudies/rec20.htm#pfpcrig>.

As parents we can understand why schools have an obsession with discipline and control. We do not like being challenged by our own kids: 'Who is the parent here?' We find it difficult to share authority with our children, so we can recognise that teachers, who are adults and often parents too, will have difficulty sharing authority with young people. We will generally accept that the world is governed by non-negotiable rules imposed by adults and that children should be punished for their misdemeanours.

It has been ever thus, so why would it change? This attitude explains why there has been so little change in schooling. It also is natural for teachers not to want to relinquish authority. There is fear that doing so would create anarchy or the simmering potential for it. And of course there is the question of results. How will we achieve successful tertiary entrance results if we cannot enforce our rules and expectations on our students? How will we guarantee safety and security if we do not have control?

These are all legitimate questions. We may believe that the world has changed and that the youth labour market is vastly different, and we may believe that our kids are different from kids of just ten years ago, but we have to trust in something. That something is still the school and the intrinsic belief that it should care for, teach and control our kids and ensure that they are disciplined enough to learn.

So, we need to make some quantum leaps in our thinking if we want to have schooling that is relevant to young people and their future. Imagine if kids in twenty years' time were still experiencing the same schooling that our kids are now! Let's take another big-picture look. Imagine our kids at 35, having left home five years earlier, with limited job prospects, who can't afford their own homes or even to start families, faced with an ageing population to support and watching wealth being generated overseas because that is where the innovative, entrepreneurial knowledge work and workers have gone. If this continues and we do not commit to major transformation then we will find that the creative, wealth-generating work will occur in countries such as Hong Kong and not Australia.

Hong Kong education system review

The Hong Kong Government has been undertaking a comprehensive review of its eduction system. The Chief Executive's Commission on Innovation and Technology Report recommends that Hong Kong invest heavily in education, paying special attention to creativity, communication skills and information technology to develop a knowledge-driven and technology-intensive economy. It suggests that education reform will take a generation to improve the quality of Hong Kong's human capital and recommends attracting talent from other places to increase its intellectual capital.

<http://www.info.gov.hk/tib/roles/second/chap3.htm>

Suddenly, we can see this small country of Australia failing to produce through its schools young people with the innovative flair, the learning disposition and skill and the excitement to make a difference. When Donald Horne wrote *The Lucky Country* in the 1960s, he warned us about complacency in the face of a global community. We are becoming complacent consumers of knowledge rather than creators of it. As baby boomers, our legacy will be a country that cannot sustain the current level of consumption and wealth. This is now evident in reduced home ownership by the under-35s, fewer children resulting in more childless or single child families, and the need for both couples in a partnership to keep working longer.

Collaboration and shared authority

The knowledge era school needs to look carefully at how to develop a culture in which there is no power struggle between teachers and young people, but rather collaboration and sharing of authority, and where both the educators and the young people they work with have a voice.

The Bolton Network Learning Community has worked innovatively on 'student voice' in schools. In their situation, student voice activities are networked. Professor David Hargreaves (2004) describes the scenario:

> At their first conference in 2003, 400 pupils from 16 schools and one independent school met … and ran workshops on a variety of themes, such as anti-bullying, peer pressure and school councils. They then decided to call themselves BLAST—Bolton Listens As Students Talk. A second conference was a consultative exercise on health and well being. This led to a review of counselling facilities; as a result a handbook was produced for all participating schools. Another development was the pupil 'learning walk', where a group of students visits other schools to see what might be learned from them and then implemented in their own home school. In one school an internal voice day led to the creation of five steering groups to take forward ideas for change.

The teachers and leaders at these schools were not afraid to share with young people, acknowledge their skills and act on their work.

The contradiction of teachers' custodial roles

Schools need to work at removing obstacles to the development of collaborative relationships between teachers and students. One of the crucial obstacles to real success in transforming schooling through relationships is that of custody. Schooling needs to separate the issue of its legal custodial role from its teaching–learning role. The two are incompatible.

Teachers find it very difficult to act as collaborators in the teaching–learning role and then as custodians in the 'duty of care' role outside the classroom. Duty of care needs to be a school responsibility rather than rest with teachers. This will require government to resource different arrangements to introduce staff with care and, in some cases, security qualifications, who would be responsible, under the school principal, for out-of-hours school care, ground supervision for recess and lunch times, bus duty, sport supervision and so on.

Traditonally teachers have always performed this custodial role. It has now been stamped into the administrative requirements of schools through legal processes and legal precedence. Parents expect that the school will assume custodial responsibility and keep their children safe and secure. School and government regulations require that teachers perform the functions associated with the custodial role from kindergarten through to Year 12. In the post-compulsory framework of the senior years there is some recognition that 'duty of care' is different. However, there are still parents who say, 'But my son/daughter is still only a child' and expect that the school will know where they are and what they are doing. While the law may be somewhat ambiguous in the post-compulsory area, a climate of anxiety has been built up in schools to the point where their custodial role has sometimes assumed precedence over their learning role.

The knowledge era school, therefore, will separate the teaching–learning role from the custodial role. The physical school needs to be seen as a typical community resource. Community laws and expectations of social behaviour need to apply. 'Community caretakers' need to assume the custodial role outside the classroom. They would be well-trained people managing young people in normal, boisterous and sometimes challenging social situations in a community facility.

Summary

Knowledge era schooling criterion 1: An attitude of sharing authority

Criterion 1 synopsis: The knowledge era school has an attitude of sharing authority, where teachers and young people are able to work together, collaborate and feel empowered together. This contrasts with the industrial era of teacher/adult control where teachers have the knowledge and power is concentrated in adult/teacher hands.

Knowledge elicitation systems	Industrial schooling
Attitude of sharing authority	Teacher control attitude
¬ teacher and young people work together to create knowledge	¬ teachers pass on knowledge
¬ people empowered	¬ power concentrated

6 | Freedom to learn

Students need a schooling environment that
will provide them with the freedom to explore, to feel
comfortable in taking risks, to develop confidence
in themselves and to find their own sense of the world.

Knowledge era schooling criterion 2:
Freedom to explore and take risks

Schools need to provide the culture that allows young people to take risks:
to have space, time and the freedom to explore.

So, let's think more about this school that shares authority. It also is a school that provides students and staff with freedom. In Australia, this was recognised as far back as the early 1970s when the Australian Capital Territory first established its senior secondary colleges, although some of this thinking was evident in the Tasmanian matriculation colleges that began in the early 1960s.

The ACT Senior Colleges for Years 11 and 12 have been developed as educational bridges between high school and pathways to further education and employment. The colleges were set up to establish a more adult-like environment where young people were treated as young adult decision-makers. Each college develops its own range of courses for students, none of which is compulsory. In a two-year period, students have the freedom and flexibility to develop their talents by designing a study program to suit their personal educational goals. They may aim to achieve a school-assessed Year 12 Certificate including a combination of accredited, tertiary accredited, vocational and registered units or they may also pursue an externally examined Tertiary Entrance Statement. Either pathway may lead to vocational certification, employment, TAFE or university entrance.

<http://www.decs.act.gov.au/schools/colleges.htm>

Students need a schooling environment that will provide them with the freedom to explore, to feel comfortable in taking risks, to develop confidence in themselves and to find their own sense of the world. We need to recognise what they have (their talents and already developed skills of learning, collaborating and teaching) and ensure that they have the schooling environment in which these talents and skills can flourish and develop further. Schools that still control young people cannot effectively create an environment in which young people can be creative, innovative or entrepreneurial.

This belief was recognised in the Australian Federal Parliamentary Inquiry (2003) into teaching, as a 'bold initiative to strengthen the quality of teaching and learning ... with fresh thinking and imaginative practice and a readiness to rethink values and to use research and reflective inquiry in shaping educational policy and practice ...' It referenced a Queensland school as a school with a commitment to creating an innovative culture.

Buranda State School, Queensland

Buranda State School is a Queensland government primary school situated on the fringe of the central business district of Brisbane, with students from a wide range of family structures and cultural, religious and socioeconomic backgrounds.

The shared vision for the school is that it should be a place where learning is creative, fun, joyful, exciting, surprising and challenging.

The adoption of philosophy as a core subject that underpins all curriculum activities has transformed the school's teaching and learning methods, By listening to each other, building on each other's ideas and accepting that there is no single right answer, children learn to be fair and open-minded, intellectually cooperative and mutually respectful. They become thoughtful and reasonable citizens.

Technology and real life learning also play an important role at Buranda School as part of a futures-oriented curriculum.

The changes at Buranda over the last six years have been far-reaching and extraordinary. Most importantly, they include demonstrable, improved student outcomes. There has also been a significant increase in enrolments, improved work practices and the development of a professional teacher learning community. The school enjoys strong support from the parent and wider communities.

> Innovation is inherently risky since no clearly set path lies ahead. In order to innovate, schools must be prepared to step into the unknown ... Building on the diverse values held by families and communities, and sharing responsibilities with them, schools can equip all young Australians to take advantage of the opportunities and themselves to become effective catalysts of change.
>
> DEST, 2003

We can feel reasonably comfortable about freedoms in a post-compulsory schooling environment with young adults, but what about students in the middle and junior years? Dobozy (1999) argues that we should learn from the success of the Montessori approach and not dismiss it because of a particular ideological perspective to their schooling. She refers to Peter Airasian (1997):

> Teachers will have to guide, not tell; to create environments in which students can make their own meanings, not be handed them by the teachers ... not stick to rigid standards and criteria; to create a safe, free, responsive environment that encourages disclosure of student construction, not a closed, judged system.
>
> Students will also have to learn new ways to perform. They have to learn to think for themselves, not wait for the teacher to tell [them] what to think; to proceed with less focus and direction from the teacher, not wait for explicit teacher direction; to express their own ideas clearly in their own words, not to answer restricted response questions; to revisit and revise constructions, not to move immediately on to the next concept or idea.
>
> But most importantly:
>
> Teachers will have to become accustomed to working with quite different and more general goals ... much of the responsibility for learning will be turned over to the students through 'hands on' experiences and activities designed to spur their construction of meaning.

Young people need the freedom to explore and take risks to become innovative. Risk-taking is trying something new and expanding one's mind and horizons, but a physical dimension is also involved, in terms of play, sport and simply exploring the environment. Some young people are into taking risks and trying new activities in a big way, but many need encouragement and opportunities created for them. This is the new world, but schools and teachers seem to take fewer risks today than thirty years ago. Parents take fewer risks too. For example, once their children walked to and from school. Now they are often taken by car. We are anxious today because of the perceived increase in threats to young people. One suspects that this is because of our greater exposure to the media, although threats through the new technologies are real and need to be managed. The following case study uses a school with a particular philosophical orientation, a Montessori school. What the school demonstrates in relation to young people needs to be seen as something that can work in any school committed to organising itself around young people.

Montessori Schooling

When Maria Montessori, founder of the Montessori educational approach, spoke about freedom, she invariably emphasised its close relationship to responsibility. To be free means to be in control of self, to be able to do what one chooses, rather than be a slave to impulse. At Cockatoo Montessori School, our way of interacting with children promotes a teacher–child relationship based on flexibility and mutual trust. High academic standards can be achieved without the need for punishments or rewards. A strong sense of responsibility and good work habits also develop without set homework. The natural consequences of their behaviour bring children to the highest form of obedience: self-discipline.

<http://www.cockatoomontessori.vic.edu.au/>

The child's liberty should have as its limits the interest of the group to which he belongs. We should therefore prevent a child from doing anything which may offend or hurt the others ... but everything else, every act that can be useful in any way whatever, may be expressed.

Maria Montessori

The other aspect of allowing our children freedom and developing their sense of responsibility is that if we do not, we are in danger of cocooning our young people. They will never develop a sense of exploring, risk-taking, being creative and solving problems if they are overprotected.

Multiple intelligences

Young people have different abilities and learn in so many different ways. They learn conceptually, visually, with their hands, through hearing and sound, through exploring and discovering, and they can combine these simultaneously. This is often referred to as 'multiple intelligences' and challenges our industrial notion of intelligence. In Chapter 3, I referred to the New City School in St Louis. Here we see a Canberra primary school committing itself to the rights of young people to have their multiple intelligences recognised.

Cook School, ACT

Cook School recognises that there are many different ways of learning and knowing and value not only the need, but also the right, of every child to learn through their own preferred learning style. Cook School is unique in not only recognising the importance of valuing each individual's learning method, but [also] implementing this through Multiple Intelligence teaching.

> Howard Gardner's Theory of Multiple Intelligence identifies that there are many forms of intelligence and that people have varying strengths and combinations of these. Gardner recognises that we communicate, learn and solve problems using at least seven forms of intelligence: Verbal/Linguistic Intelligence, Logical/Mathematical Intelligence, Visual/Spatial Intelligence, Musical/Rhythmic Intelligence, Kinaesthetic Intelligence, Interpersonal Intelligence and Intrapersonal Intelligence.
>
> This theory is seen at Cook School to be an ideal framework to use in ensuring good teaching practices and improved results for students. This multiple choice approach to teaching is based on the community's strong sense of social justice and belief that all children should be given opportunities to stay on their own preferred paths to excellence.
>
> <http://www.cookps.act.edu.au/>

If we define being intelligent as having the capability to perform well academically then only a small number of young people fit this category. However, if we broaden our perspective, we see many more young people as being very intelligent. A very good example of this is in relation to information technology. Many young people, predominantly boys, can work intuitively with computers, web design and construction, programming and multimedia work with such ease that we should be humbled by them. Yet, in traditional academic terms these abilities rarely rate a mention. Two young men from Eltham College have been recognised in the top five students in Australia for their multimedia work, but in traditional academic terms they would not be recognised in such manner.

Respecting young people

Young people do not come to school deficient as learners. In fact their learning skills and the information they have makes them accomplished learners. The knowledge era school recognises these abilities and builds a sound well-rounded education for each individual. It allows students to tap into the talents, knowledge and wisdom of teachers while being given the environment to pursue the areas in which they have a high degree of aptitude. This involves working together, collaborating, recognising and working with the multiple talents of young people. Secondary schools could learn much about this supportive environment at the kindergarten at Lauriston Girls' School.

Lauriston Girls' School, Victoria

> At the kindergarten at Lauriston Girls' School, the Reggio Emilia concept is a strong influence throughout the kindergarten programs and provides an emphasis on play, being happy and developing at an appropriate pace. Our children go home happy and are eager to return the following day.

The Reggio Emilia approach is guiding many early learning centres in developing their own eclectic approach to working with young people. In Chapter 4, I made reference to the relevance of this and other learning theories in developing more substantial approaches to scaffolding learning throughout schooling.

Not too many years ago young people were regarded as empty vessels to be filled with knowledge and skills that only teachers were deemed to possess. Most young people accepted this situation until the end of compulsory schooling when they left for one of the many available jobs. Students were managed in classes because they could all receive the knowledge at the same time and in the same way. If students did not pick up knowledge quickly they were regarded as not academic or as slower learners. They could leave to successfully pursue work or technical training. Now, leaving school early epitomises failure and this dated scenario still applies in many schools today. At a South Australian primary school, however, they have developed a culture that says they will not accept a notion of failure.

Elizabeth North Primary School, SA

'We can achieve'—Focus on literacy brings success to Elizabeth North Students—Commonwealth

Designated as a disadvantaged school, Elizabeth North Primary school in Adelaide's northern suburbs has a high proportion of students with learning difficulties, children with significant intellectual and physical disabilities, and a large population of Aboriginal children and children with language backgrounds other than English.

While he admits that teaching this wide spectrum of children represents a challenge to staff, principal Dick D'Aloia says it's not good enough to expect that some of these children will fail.

'For too long people thought that children in disadvantaged schools didn't have much chance. We as a staff have high but realistic expectations: we know that the students can achieve and never accept what is second class if we know they can do better.

'Equally important,' he says, 'has been providing extra support to those students who need it.

'About four years ago we set about making our classes smaller for about seven hours a week. This has meant that teachers could attend more to children's individual needs,' said Mr D'Aloia. This is particularly important in junior primary, because if

> children haven't mastered basic skills and concepts at that stage, they will experience further failure.'
>
> The focus in these smaller classes has been on literacy. Said Mr D'Aloia, 'Literacy is the highest need of our students here: to speak, to read, to verbalise.'
>
> According to Mr D'Aloia, the program has helped to develop a culture in the school that says, 'we can achieve'—a community perspective that is shared by students and teachers alike.
>
> For further information, including details on the target group and responsible agency, follow the link to Initiatives Targeting Recommendation 17 at <http://www.mceetya.edu.au/stepping/casestudies/rec17.htm#poip>.

Knowledge era schooling concerns all young people. It is not a class concept, nor does it simply apply specifically to Western cultures. It should work as well within the supportive culture of Elizabeth North Primary as at Eltham College.

Today students come to school with access to information and learning skills that should make them partners in the learning process. This gives them a right to a different status: one that suggests that learning involves working together with their teachers and collaborating in the learning process.

Flexible structures promote innovation

School organisational structures need to be flexible and student-centred. These structures need to provide:

- an environment that challenges students
- time for students to explore and work at a pace appropriate to them
- for different student groupings depending on the learning circumstance and student state of readiness
- a great sense of security for students to express themselves, to explore and take risks with learning.

Rather than structures in the strict sense of their meaning in schools, it concerns the culture or climate of the school. Schools can have their own structures to suit the way in which they wish to operate, provided that the culture allows the freedom for students to explore, take risks, feel good about themselves, work with others, be challenged at and above their abilities, develop their areas of interest and take time to achieve results.

Structure should emerge from mission and culture. Schools, however, tend to have established rigid structures that have proven to be very effective barriers to innovation and change. Existing structures should be challenged in relation to how much they support student ownership and self-direction. Above all, structure needs to be student-centred not school- or teacher-centred. School- and teacher-centred schools tend to be dominated by efficiency and management control.

Too often school governance arrangements are determined by the demands of the next level in the schooling–post-schooling chain. For example, the demands of final schooling credentialing and tertiary entrance tend to determine the way in which senior schooling is structured. In Victoria, the VCE and ENTER score demands, coupled with media pressure and parental expectations, have a greater influence on how schools structure learning than any real belief in what should constitute innovative senior schooling for young adults. This, of course, flows to the middle years and how they are structured and managed. The external influences on schools need to be addressed to help motivate real change in schools.

Student voice

Students need to be empowered and feel that they can make a difference to their school community. Decision-making structures at a whole-school level need to involve students who also need to be able to work collaboratively with their teachers in making decisions about learning activities.

Students at Eltham College are involved in the strategic direction process of the College Board. Each year the Board invites the school captains to participate in their strategic planning workshop, which is held over two days. The students' contribution is as valued as that of any other member of the Board. They do not participate in decisions about staff, although the school involves members of the Student Council in staff selection processes.

The following case study is a systemic one from Canada and illustrates how systems, groups of schools and indeed individual schools can rise to the challenge of young people's need for voice.

Student voice: The voices of today and tomorrow

... Students will provide the momentum and energy for change if they know the support is there. You can build momentum through student excitement.

Youth Member, Manitoba School Improvement Program Advisory Committee

The Canadian-based Manitoba School Improvement Program Inc. (MSIP) has evolved since 1991 as a multifaceted improvement network of public secondary schools. Through action research and student-centered initiatives, MSIP has developed a vision in which 'student voice' is pivotal to improving high schools and student learning outcomes.

The independent organisation emphasises collaborative school cultures within a school-centred, community partnership-oriented perspective. MSIP has encouraged schools to include students in their improvement efforts, with the ultimate goal of creating better conditions for student learning and engagement.

The experiences of MSIP schools suggest that students can provide both pressure and support for the change process, particularly when they work with dedicated teachers in their own schools on issues of common interest. MSIP has learned that where there is a voice there must be a listener. In order for students to be involved

> actively in their learning, decision-makers must be prepared to listen, respond and make changes to their policy.
>
> The Making a Choice! Raise your Voice Conference is one example of a MSIP initiative. It is attended annually by 300 students, province-wide, with the aim of placing student voice issues at the centre of school reform efforts.
>
> Documented results of MSIP initiatives (Earl & Lee, 1998) include improved academic performance, increased student enrolment, increased family and community involvement in schools, reduced disciplinary incidents, improved class attendance and increased student graduations.
>
> Pekrul, 2004, The Manitoba School Improvement Program Inc. Winnipeg, Manitoba, Canada

A student-centred environment

The intention to change at Eltham College was established through Strategic Planning 2000 and actions were put in place that ensured that people would have to take up new behaviours. One of the important changes was recognition by staff that the college had moved from an adult-centred to a student-centred environment. The second year of change intensified the pace, the emphasis still on learning to teach for self-direction and within a context that the world of today's young people was very different.

Parents and teachers needed to be convinced that the world had changed and young people were changing with it, and that it is not simply a passing phase. The simple Game Boy illustration from Chapter 1 certainly had people thinking hard about this generation of young people and their capacity as learners, teachers and team players.

We in schools need to share the triumphs of young people and their schools and consider how we evaluate these successes. We need to develop improved reporting processes for parents and the community to better understand what young people are achieving. We need media that will continue to tell the 'good news education' stories about young people. Without these, people have only such measures as senior school results, and these are totally inadequate to convey the real outcomes of schooling.

The community needs to be convinced that the great majority of young people can be trusted and that schools do not have to be focused on control and management. The community needs to be persuaded that young people can handle freedom and be risk-takers. The community needs to understand that developing an innovative culture does not mean experimenting with young people. Years of research and practice should be used to show people that this is not experimentation, but putting together our knowledge and experience, gathered over many years, to create schooling that is relevant to the modern age (Caldwell, 2004).

The students interviewed in the Flinders University study (Slade, 2001) said:

> The people who have got control are the ones who have to change; have to give up being control freaks, seein' everything the way they want to … Anyway, the ones

who do well at school are the ones who are like the teachers. In twenty years they'll be running the schools and nothin' will have changed—except most of them will be women. But that's no big difference. A control freak's a control freak. Men or women, doesn't matter.

Slade goes on to suggest:

Despite research, current or new strategies, and the best of intentions, nothing will ever change until … the teachers, the school culture and a credentialing process that supports and reproduces a particular kind of teacher, are changed.

But, the students caution:

… They don't want to listen … They make the rules … There is always an excuse … Maybe the students aren't always wrong.

We have continued the practice of developing and running schools to suit the needs of adults, teachers and parents. These needs are best summed up as controlled learning and highly supervised work spaces, dominated by a fear of litigation and also a fear of losing control to the students, particularly boys.

We live in a world that increasingly values people who are self-starters and entrepreneurial risk-takers who use creative initiative. At times we listen too much to the people associated with the public service and the increasingly fewer large enterprises. These bodies tend to focus more on industrial work values and highly supervised environments. Most people work in small business. Increasingly young people will be small business operators, possibly as independent contractors. To prosper they will need to be comfortable and confident with change and have the skills referred to in this chapter.

Freedom

Young people, therefore, need developmentally appropriate freedom. Freedom is an interesting word. It is the cornerstone of our beliefs in democracy, but we are very careful with it in schools. Without increased freedom in our schools, young people will always be in conflict with school and will not develop the disposition and skills needed to make a difference in the 21st century. Freedom does not mean a laissez-faire environment with 'kids running wild', but rather an increasingly adult environment where young people start to make important decisions about themselves and their behaviour, distinguishing right from wrong and shaping their own futures. The normal responsibilities arising from community expectation and law and order should prevail as in general society. However, within these parameters, young people should have considerable freedom to learn to make decisions. Knowledge era schooling provides the ability to explore the world responsibly and with good judgment. Young people learn, over time, to make good choices.

Summary

Knowledge era schooling Criterion 2: Freedom to explore and take risks

Criterion 2 synopsis: The knowledge era school needs to provide a culture in which there is freedom to explore and take risks. Both older and younger people need these opportunities and this level of respect to be able to scaffold learning through a diminishing adult role as young people assume greater independence. The culture that controls teachers and insists that teachers control the learning process is industrial and clearly belongs to another time. Young people need the freedom to take risks and have the time and space within which to do it. Teachers need to move from the inflexibility of time and space within a four-walled classroom culture. Teachers and parents need to recognise that the learning needed for success in the knowledge era cannot occur when young people are mollycoddled and cocooned.

Knowledge elicitation systems	Industrial schooling
Freedom to explore and take risks	Controlled environment where teachers manage learning
¬ young people have space and time to learn	¬ inflexible time and space in closed classrooms

Change embedded in the culture | 7

Schools can deliberately set out to embed change in
their culture and they can be sensitive to the world and
'read and flex' with it. They need to deliberately create
a culture of change where young people can feel not
only part of it, but also contribute to it.

Knowledge era schooling criterion 3:
A culture of change

The development of a culture of change in schooling is imperative. Change
needs to be central to all that young people experience in school because
through it young people will develop resiliency, adaptability and personal
flexibility to become not only people who can cope with change but also
agents of it.

Change needs to be part of the culture of school. When, for example, the Australian
Capital Territory set up its senior colleges, it recognised that students would arrive
each year from their junior high schools with the same behaviours, attitudes and
need to 'flex their muscles'. They understood that entering students would need to
learn to become creative young adults. They would require an environment that
accepted change. The senior college staff had to become resilient because a change
culture involves more than learning from one group a range of procedures and

policies to make the environment more controllable for teachers: it is a continual collaborative process undertaken with the students. That was 33 years ago and a visit to any of the colleges today shows that they not only still have the same beliefs, but also provide an environment of greater freedom for their students.

When the Queensland senior colleges were established they used the Technical And Further Education (TAFE) culture as a model. In the TAFE culture, young people were treated much more as adults: they were free to come and go when classes were not on. Consequences were simple: if students did not turn up for class, or the work was not done, they were given a chance to explain themselves and rectify the problem, but if they continued to abuse this freedom, they failed (Warner in Seddon and Deer, 1992). They were able to move from a teacher culture of caring, in which teachers accept all responsibility and do much of the work, to one in which the young adults can assume increasing ownership of their own living and working.

The knowledge era school culture encourages self-management. It is a culture that rejects the routines that characterise industrial, teacher-controlled classroom cultures. Research that commenced in the mid-1970s directed our attention to the routinised nature of schools and classrooms (Warner, 1987). Routines do not foster change because change reduces the comfort level of schools and encourages greater authority and control. In so many ways, it is not simply the knowledge era that has challenged traditional schooling. Young people have been challenging it for many years because they have believed that they deserve more than being in a controlled, authoritarian environment.

As senior colleges and senior secondary colleges developed (for example, St Mary's, Bendigo Secondary College and Geelong Senior Secondary College), campus-oriented and adult-like environments were established. But of greater significance to their students, these colleges embraced the real world. The real world of industry and business was being transformed and this interaction helped create better change cultures in the colleges. They could not, indeed did not want, to settle into a safe, comfortable zone again. With their students, they engaged much more closely with the real world. Ringwood Secondary College in Victoria, as previously mentioned, has followed this lead and it shows exemplary practice in its interactions with the real world of industry change.

However, the embedding of change in the culture of a school must affect the student culture within the school. Young people need to see that learning is about changing and that new learning is created by change. The relationship between their schooling and the world to which they belong needs to reflect the realities of a rapidly transforming world. The young person who comes to school the day after a parent has been made redundant does not need an inflexible school ethos, but rather one that will respond to the individual needs of that student.

Schools can deliberately set out to embed change in their culture and they can be sensitive to the world and 'read and flex' with it. They need to deliberately create a culture of change where young people can not only feel part of it, but also contribute to it.

A new Specialist Trust School in Essex, England, set out as a greenfield site to create a culture that embedded change.

Chafford Hundred Campus, UK

In creating a new school which opened in 2001, the staff of Chafford Hundred Campus had the opportunity to re-think conventional approaches to teaching and learning, the curriculum, ethos and structures. Its belief was that any school wishing to wear the mantle of 'school of the future' needed the ability and willingness to look critically at the old accepted ways and would be willing to take on board new knowledge and deal with old (and new) problems.

The ethos of Chafford Hundred Campus is to meet the needs of the individual in the 21st century. The term 'campus' alone signals its uniqueness as an institution, as it brings together under one roof a nursery, a primary school, a secondary school, adult education, a public library and facilities for the community at large.

Chafford Hundred Campus is also one of the first eight schools to work with the RSA (Royal Society of Arts) to pilot a new curriculum, the aim being to redefine schooling and open the minds of young people in the 21st century. This was prompted by the opinion of many, particularly employers, that the National Curriculum does not equip young people with the skills essential for everyday life.

One of the most influential advocates of this argument is Howard Gardner, who suggests that people with apparently sophisticated knowledge of a subject often fail to apply it effectively when they encounter problems whose form or context is unknown to them. The RSA Curriculum, on the other hand, is founded on five competencies that will equip young people with the essential life skills.

<http://www.chaffordhundredcampus.thurrock.sch.uk/article.php?a=26>

Schools are well practised at weathering the storms of change long enough not to have to move too far from their comfort zones of adult control. It is essential that the future knowledge era schools ensure that their teachers believe that change is a permanent reality.

Teachers who model the real world

One of the critical areas in which the knowledge era school can create opportunities for ownership of change and innovation is within the staff structure. To create a fluid environment in which change can be enacted smoothly and new learning can be passed on quickly, teachers in the knowledge era school need to have ownership of their jobs and feel empowered to work innovatively with young people. To achieve this, staff management structures must be relatively non-hierarchical and flexible. Structures need to be able to alter quickly to embrace changing circumstances.

The Eltham College experience—certified agreements

One of the early and most difficult changes made at Eltham College when it first embarked on its knowledge era school reforms was to remove heads of department or teacher supervisors and replace them with individual teacher ownership within a team context. Performance development processes for each individual support this innovation. Teachers have to learn to be self-directed and collaborative, reflecting the skills and attitudes we seek to develop with our students. Executive leadership should be non-hierarchical but functional relative to the particular area of responsibility, as for example, Student Services, Learning and Curriculum Development, Human Resources and Teaching.

Further to this macro restructuring, to motivate teachers to adopt this new learning approach, the knowledge era school offers its staff the option of a more dynamic remuneration package than the standard incremental annual increase for ten years (at which point a teacher's salary is capped). At Eltham College, senior management negotiated with staff representatives over an 18-month period to create a certified agreement—a remuneration package that can be taken up by any of the college staff. The certified agreement created a professionally driven program to encourage and reward employee excellence. This shift in incentive and rewarding teacher professionalism has been recognised as one of the keys to creating a school for a knowledge-intensive society, and is based on sound professional practice found in other industries.

It is incumbent on the knowledge era school to provide sufficient incentive to stimulate outstanding teaching performance, and reward exemplary employees who demonstrate leadership, initiative, and mentoring of other staff. Teachers now have the opportunity to earn what they deserve.

The essence of the new certified agreement defines three bands of teaching practice:

- Band 1: new or relatively inexperienced employees, needing mentoring support
- Band 2: relatively experienced employees
- Band 3: employees who demonstrate exemplary practice and who exhibit excellence in mentoring and leadership.

Exemplar status is not a permanent position. Maintaining the position is contingent on continued performance in the role. Staff at all levels are reviewed by a panel of four staff members, two of whom are selected by the employees. Eltham College staff recognised as leaders and mentors within the school have the potential to increase their income each year.

Within the context of these new arrangements, where initiative and fresh thinking are recognised and rewarded, teachers need to know that it is all right to make mistakes— that is, to take risks. Senior management at Eltham College works on the principle that if the initiative is within the college's strategic directions—that is, it is right for young people, meets with its values, and is within budget—then it should be supported.

Teachers need to know and understand the mission and strategic directions of their school and to see these reflected within the language and behaviour of senior staff. Senior staff members need to be available to support teachers, help them work through their ideas, access resources and acknowledge them and their efforts.

Teachers have incredible skills, but have not always been free to use them. They need both the sense of freedom (and, therefore, a belief that they are supported) and the opportunity to use it. Many also need assistance to identify their skills and to articulate them, as often teachers have not recognised what makes them effective.

For some teachers, giving away established methods of classroom management and control, working without some of the school-based trappings of 'discipline' support and actually trusting that students will respond, may feel like stepping into a void. They have to trust that they will be supported. They have to trust that they will not be exposed through unfair and untimely evaluations, but that they will be acknowledged for what they have achieved. These relate to the new teaching culture of the knowledge era school.

Considerable effort from schooling leadership is needed to establish this culture with teachers, particularly when there has been significant staff change (for example, the abolition of heads of department). Abolishing established positions, and placing responsibility on teachers and teams encourages the belief that the school is serious about change. It helps emphasise that schools are for young people with teachers who believe in working with them.

Summary

Knowledge era school criterion 3: A culture of change

Criterion 3 synopsis: The knowledge era school has change as part of its culture, in contrast to the industrial school where the structures of control are change-averse. A culture of change helps develop resiliency, independence, adaptability and innovation. It is in stark contrast to the industrial school that fosters uniformity, compliance and dependence.

Knowledge era schooling	Industrial schooling
Change is part of the culture	Highly structured and change-averse
¬ develops resiliency	¬ fosters only limited coping skills, inflexible
¬ develops independence	¬ fosters compliance, rigidity
¬ develops adaptability	¬ fosters only managed innovation

¬ develops creativity and innovation	¬ is supervisory
¬ is entrepreneurial	¬ ignores opportunity and risk-taking

There is a very large difference between industrial schools, which dominated the education landscape for the whole of the 20th century, and the knowledge era school for the young people of the 21st-century world.

Rethinking attitudes and roles | 8

In Australia, the unrelenting focus on tertiary entrance scores
is a constraining influence on genuine school transformation.
It influences the maintenance of traditional school subject
curriculum and focuses middle years teaching and learning
on preparation for the senior years and tertiary entrance type
assessment. It influences how schools operate; it produces
'preparing for exams' rather than self-directed learning; it
causes strict management and control. It, above all, is a very
strong deterrent to transformation.

Knowledge era schooling criterion 4:
Modelling the 21st century in schools

Schools should be able to model the world that young people know and in
which they live and will work. This includes a willingness to revisit what
knowledge means in a schooling context and to acknowledge that there is
not only academic intelligence but also multiple intelligences, and individual
talents can operate in a social, collaborative sense. Knowledge era schooling
encourages academic and vocational education to converge.

Knowledge era schooling challenges schools and their teachers. It creates an inherent
threat to established authority and role definitions, which have traditionally been
used to manage large groups of young people—a daunting task at any time, never

mind when faced with a generation such as this one! Knowledge era schooling is vastly different from traditional schooling. It requires attitudes and behaviours of young people and teachers that have not been part of their previous shared schooling experiences.

As long ago as 1968, in the educational classic *Life in classrooms,* Philip Jackson described the very busy, unpredictable environment of a normal classroom as having 'up to one thousand different interactions a day'. Classrooms have always been intense environments, which gave rise to management rather than exploration.

With the move to a more student-centred curriculum within the knowledge era school and its greater choice of learning activities, we need to develop a learning environment that allows for more individual interaction with the teacher and individual education programs or customisation.

Traditional classroom thinking

Research from the 1980s into teacher and student thinking (Warner, 1987) in classrooms described how routines rather than decisions characterised teachers in class. It also directed attention to the manipulative thinking in which students engaged. Teaching in traditional classrooms and schools is difficult because teachers have to manage up to thirty young people while teaching them something from an assessable curriculum. As a teacher who has some experience and has mastered the routines, the last thing you want to do is have these challenged.

However, over the past few years, young people have been challenging this traditional schooling environment. They realise that they have skills and information not possessed by their teachers as well as recognising that what schools offer is increasingly irrelevant to their emerging world. In schools, the leadership challenge has tended to come in aggressive forms from young men but we will also experience more intolerance from young women in the not too distant future as they too recognise the disconnection between schooling, living and working.

This crucial issue of the future rather than the past is cleverly described by leading Australian education academic Professor Hedley Beare who put forward the voice of Angelica, whom we first met in Chapter 3. She continues her description of her vision of her life.

I AM THE FUTURE'S CHILD

... On present life expectancy, I will live until I am over 80. I will be alive and well into the 2070s and my children will live to see the twenty-second century. Can you imagine what the world will be like for them?

Only three of every hundred babies born this year live in developed countries. So wherever I live or work, I will certainly be mixing in a multinational, multi-cultural and multi-faith setting, and white people could be the ethnic minorities. I will have to think about that when I prepare for a job ...

... The Asia/Pacific area will be a strong focus of my world. China already has a population ten times that of Japan, and nearly half a billion Chinese are under the age of 25. The Asian continent (from India to Japan) already accounts for half the world's population. A Hong Kong bank advertises now, 'There are three billion people in Asia. Half of them are under 25. Consider it a growing market.' Those under-25s are my contemporaries. They will be very aggressive in a number of ways, good and bad, over the next few decades.

It will not matter what nationality I have, because my world is smaller, people move about, and most workplaces will be internationalised. My world is likely to be borderless. I will have access to the world economy through credit cards and trans-national banks, and it will be easy to travel overseas …

… I do not expect to spend all my life in the employment of one company. No company is likely to remain unchanged for that long anyway. For me, 'work' will ebb and flow, and will often be done intensively, in large chunks in a short period of time. I will manage my own career, and I will not leave it to a company or an organisation to do it for me. I may change jobs or relocate seventeen or so times during my working life, and at least three of those changes will be major ones. My husband and I will have to juggle jobs and careers, perhaps in different locations …

… In a world like this, it is important for me to know what I stand for. I will look to my school to help me form my values and decide on my system of beliefs. I have to be careful about what I believe and what I take for granted without thinking. I am not sure where my mother and father picked up their beliefs and attitudes. Our family doesn't go to church, tabernacle or temple any more. There is not much religion in my home. I'll have to be more systematic and deliberate about it because of the complex world I will function in …

… I already learn as much from television as I do from school. I spend more time with TV than I do with my teachers. I watch each year about 1400 hours of TV and see 22 000 commercials which tell me what I should value, what I should eat and what sort of behaviour is acceptable. During my time as a student, then, attempts will be made to reconcile TV viewing and education, even to blur the boundaries between them …

… The way we use computers is gently refashioning what my generation thinks about knowledge—what it is, how it is accessed, how knowledge is produced, who owns it. 'Finding out about things' is taking on new meanings and methods for us … I am connected to the Internet, I have my own email address, and some of my teachers will be located overseas …

Computers are changing the way my schooling is arranged. We have access to an enormous amount of information, and we can consult almost any library and government department in the world. We can find out things through the computer that even our teachers know little about. So we have a different view about knowledge and studying.

The old way of learning—by steps and stages, by the sequencing of learning into one best path, by the traditional, scientific approaches, by having the curriculum divided neatly into subjects—is already passing. Knowledge for me is a web of interconnections where I access interesting information from many angles. Words like 'subjects', 'classes', 'grades' and 'promotion' do not make much sense to me. Schools will not be organised that way by the time I leave primary education …

… I will not sit for 'final examinations' at the end of my last year at school. That seems a rather silly notion to me. My performance as a student will be routinely checked against national and international benchmarks throughout my schooling. I can choose my assessments and which certificates I present for. The really good universities in the world are all international, and are not restricted by the country they happen to be located within. I want to study in a university or college like that …

… My name is Angelica. I am 5 years old. And I am sitting in one of your classrooms today.

Beare, 2001

Professor Beare's analysis is real and should inspire us to develop a knowledge era school for every Angelica. Her present school, based in the past, will not take her successfully into her future.

The obstacles to change in schooling

Beyond educators' delayed recognition of the need for drastic change in schooling, there is a range of serious issues that are impediments to wholesale transformation in schools.

During a visit to the United Kingdom in 2004, I spent time talking with the editor of a major metropolitan daily newspaper who, like me, has two young children. Her priorities centred on obtaining the results to get into university and she believed that disruptive students made it more difficult. She saw innovation in traditional terms, but recognised the contradictions for her children who were 'children of the knowledge era'. Even for young educated parents, the concept of change in schooling is very difficult. We tend to opt for what we are comfortable with and hope it pays off, rather than actually demanding that schools change for our children.

Government attitudes

The failure of governments to provide sufficient post-school opportunities for young people is influential in ensuring that parents and the community react negatively to change in schools. It is a wonderful strategy for maintaining schooling as it is. In the United Kingdom, rather than look at the issue of available places or reviewing other approaches to providing post-school education and training, the government is considering how it can introduce further discrimination within the A levels, taking a path that is more exclusionary than ever.

In Australia, the unrelenting focus on tertiary entrance scores is a constraining influence on genuine school transformation. It influences the maintenance of traditional school subject curriculum and focuses middle years teaching and learning on preparation for the senior years and tertiary entrance type assessment. It influences how schools operate; it produces 'preparing for exams' rather than self-directed learning; it causes strict management and control. It, above all, is a very strong deterrent to transformation.

For too long, countries such as Australia and the United Kingdom have maintained an educational hierarchy that progressively reduces available places at subsequent levels of education. In the United States there has been a long-term strategy of placing as many school graduates as possible into post-school college. This accounts, in part, for a society that is far more articulate and capable of understanding the more complex issues that it is presented with. Despite the tendency to be somewhat inwardly focused, the United States has been successful in producing a more innovative learning culture on a massive scale, notwithstanding the widely recognised inequalities in American society.

The need for a national approach

Another enormous impediment to change is that Australia has a small population within six states and two territories, and a federal government with few powers in relation to education. Education is seen as a state's responsibility. To achieve genuine national change we, working together in society, have to model what we expect of our young people. Many individual schools will change, but how much stronger would our schools be if we took a united, collaborative national approach?

The complexity of classroom teaching associated with the not-inconsiderable task of managing schools with several hundred up to several thousand students is another of the major reasons why schools have been slow to change. Instead, educators, from academics in education faculties in universities to teachers at schools, have traditionally focused on curriculum changes, causing minimal disruption to management and control than would be required for a school culture shift.

The curriculum can be described as the planned subject content and learning activities generally prescribed by external agencies such as the Victorian Curriculum and Assessment Authority or the Queensland Studies Authority. For some decades now there has been freedom to select topics and activities from within the prescribed curriculum. Most school curriculum change has involved additions to deal with new issues that emerge in society—for example, sex education, environmental studies, business and money management, driver education and so on.

Schools attempting strategic change or transformation have been labelled non-mainstream or alternative. Such labelling protects the traditional school, particularly the selective government and non-government school, and its standard approach to managing the school and its young people. Forums that should inspire discussion of new possibilities often inhibit free flow of ideas by treating the potential innovator as radical and on the fringe.

Fear of loss of control

Overall, however, the biggest obstacle to change in schooling has been the fear of losing control over students. There are few better examples of this than the cries from teaching unions and, to some extent, the media, for increased powers to discipline, suspend and expel 'unruly' students. Political parties also amplify this theme during elections. They tend to make a range of promises to give schools and teachers greater disciplinary powers. The anti-social behaviour issue is one that the media generate across most countries. They report system responses, trying to deal with the symptoms rather than the causes. For example, the media tend to lay blame on students for issues such as teacher stress.

Authorities, teacher educators and education researchers, schools and media lay the blame for young people's anti-social behaviour at many doors. However, virtually no one queries the relationship between our existing schools and the new world young people inhabit. It is not seen as a cause for anti-social behaviour. This does not excuse anti-social behaviour but does help explain why it might exist and why it might get much worse if we do not substantially change our schools and their teacher–student interactions.

We cannot continue to blame young people for anti-social behaviour. Teachers can show equally abhorrent anti-social attitudes towards some young people. There is a causal relationship between the severity of student anti-social behaviour and teacher attitudes and behaviour towards them (Slade, 2001). Slade (2001) reports a student as saying:

> If you get teachers that are really good, you can chat with them, have a good lesson, then you tend to get more work done. With teachers that are pricks to you, you tend not to like them, not try as hard, retaliate against them … I reckon that boys are leaving school because of the teachers … you get pissed off with the teachers and just think 'might as well leave'.

Many of these young people are being turned off learning by their experiences with schooling. It is not just a few 'troublemakers', but a significant number of young women and more often young men. These are young people with a wide range of talents and skills who may well give up on being the learners they need to be to successfully negotiate the challenges of living and working in the 21st century. As parents, we need to continue to ask loudly and often why we still allow schools to alienate young people.

We cannot continue to allow young people to disengage in the middle years of school (Years 5–9). Maybe as parents we are sometimes guilty of thinking, 'I wish our school would let the disruptive students go so the others can get on with their work.' But what if our child is the disruptive one? Most schools, when pressed, would agree that these 'troublemakers' are often bright young people with untapped potential.

In reporting his discussions with some 1800 young people, Slade (2001) said:

> Authoritarian school policies and practices, together with what the boys believe are unachievable behaviour expectations, ensure that this response to 'bad teachers'

becomes a downward spiral of disaffection, resistance, resentment, anger and retaliation. For some, it becomes retaliation at any cost.

Young people in the middle years create real fear of change in teachers and schools. Creating a 'working-together environment' with 5- to 10-year-olds is different from creating one with 11- to 14-year-olds and if no collaborative relationship exists by then, making this work with 15- to 18-year-olds is daunting. We know that schools with authoritarian discipline, detentions, bells and structures aren't working for many young people, but we won't take up the challenge of changing it because of our fear of a potential breakdown in 'discipline'. The reality is that this breakdown has occurred.

Towards transformation

Nearly twenty years ago, when I was involved in developing the first combined senior school–TAFE senior colleges in Queensland I recall that local high schools were glad to be rid of their 'troublemakers', but not so happy when many of their more 'promising' students opted to study at the senior colleges because of the changed, student-centred culture. Twenty years ago, young post-compulsory students were ready to work as young adults with teachers who also were prepared to work with them. We offered both the environment and an integrated academic and vocational curriculum and young people succeeded (Smith and Cranston, 1988; Seddon and Deer, 1992).

It can be done. Young people and teachers can learn to work together. This reminds me of a poem from *The geranium on the windowsill just died, but teacher you went right on* by Albert Cullum:

> *Teacher, come on outside!*
> *I'll race you to the see-saw!*
> *No, you won't fall off!*
> *I'll show you how!*
> *Don't be afraid, teacher.*
> *Grab my hand and follow me.*
> *You can learn all over again!*

Nevertheless, substantial transformation of the schooling system is a huge hurdle to jump and, as with the custodial issue, it requires significant commitment from policy makers and schools.

Young people too have been socialised into having expectations of 'how schools are meant to operate and how teachers and students should relate'. When confronted by a new regime or teachers with different attitudes, who might try new things and provide greater freedoms, their initial reaction is to take advantage of the reduced restrictions rather than greeting them with participatory enthusiasm.

Many years ago, when I was in teacher education and involved in research, I interviewed an experienced teacher who said, 'I tried to be innovative once, but never again. I spent weeks preparing new resources and then a weekend setting up the classroom. When they arrived on Monday morning they went wild. They were not interested.'

Of course things like this will happen unless students are involved, brought into the process and given the chance to assume some ownership and then taught to work with the initiative. At Eltham College, one of the early difficulties we had with the new concept of teaching learners to be self-directed were teachers who thought, 'So they're meant to be self-directed now. Well, in that case, as teachers, we'd better step back and watch them sink or swim.'

Some teachers at Eltham College tried to enlist students (and their parents) in their support against the notion of self-direction. I remember walking around the college with a Year 12 student, who wanted to talk to me about the effects the changes were having on his teachers. He had been convinced that the effects were detrimental. He was angry but reasonable and we talked it through and developed a relationship where he and his friends would come and share their issues. He graduated with good results, and feeling positive. His two younger brothers have also successfully become self-directed and risk-takers with good results thrown in!

Young people are not dissimilar to adults. The vast majority of them can be trusted and do not need restrictive laws and enforcement officers. Yet, in schools we tend to behave on the basis that if a few cannot be trusted then we will not trust anyone. Some teachers use this method in their classes and school principals are notorious for using a 'whole school is to blame' mentality. We are all familiar with the line, 'If the person responsible doesn't own up, you will all stay in at lunch time' or rules set to deal with one or two students but applied to everyone in the class.

Instead of using the exception rule to deal with students who have or create problems, we impose a fairly autocratic regime over all students to try to prevent the problems. However, as Slade's (2001) young interviewees in the Flinders University study suggest, this only exacerbates the problems. Slade says, 'They were far less prepared to see compliance as a possible strategy to slow down the spiral of disaffection.' In relating it to boys, both in single-sex and co-educational schools, they 'uniformly stressed the failure of adults to accept difference, claiming that most boys are treated unfavourably because they are not the "preferred" student type'.

Transformation not modification

There are exciting programs working in schools that address some of the issues of student alienation. Clearly, principles of collaboration and networking are central. Maleny State High School Flexi School in Queensland shows that cultures that engage alienated young people can be developed. The unfortunate issue with this illustration is that too often we think in terms of alternatives rather than the mainstream. We should ask why this program is not part of the full high school program.

Maleny State High School Flexi School, Queensland

Since 1999 the Maleny State High School Flexi School has been working with alienated young people who express their dissatisfaction by leaving school or by displaying inappropriate behaviour within the traditional school system.

The Flexi School has the support of Education Queensland, which provides a teacher for the school as well as access to Maleny State High School facilities and resources. The school also relies on services and resources provided by the community.

The school offers a variety of education program options. Students can opt to do subjects through distance education, link to the high school, complete programs developed at the Flexi school or develop independent projects. There is also the Three-Up School-in-Work Program involving a young person, a mentor and a workplace host enabling young people to develop vocational education knowledge and skills in the workplace.

The school plays a vital role in assisting some young people to complete their secondary schooling, become self-motivated, self-directed learners and helping them to develop the self-confidence and skills required to make a more effective contribution to the community. For further information, including details on the target group and responsible agency, follow the link to Initiatives targeting Recommendation 21 at <http://www.mceetya.edu.au/stepping/casestudies/rec21.htm#mfs>.

Australian educators should focus on where fundamental change can be implemented. They should create new conditions that will allow us to arrive at our new destination of a competitive Australian economy in a globalised marketplace and then work with people to help them deal with the changes.

Incremental change: a barrier to transformation

The notion of letting change evolve, as many school leaders and educators argue, only allows the change to be incorporated into the dominant culture—that is, we keep it all well managed and controlled. A good example of this is the introduction of vocational education into senior schooling on an equal footing with the academic curriculum. This happened first in Queensland in 1986, followed shortly after by Canberra's senior colleges. Future physicists did Automotive. Year 10 dropouts from school went on to do diplomas in Hospitality Management. English teachers learned to teach Communication without Shakespeare and Maths teachers taught Maths to Furniture students. They all used first names, never had assemblies and got together to solve problems. Almost twenty years later, Victoria introduced a Certificate of Applied Learning because the system would not accept the convergence of academic and vocational curriculum, and schooling for seniors remains academically controlled.

Incremental change and single focus innovations do not result in transformation. Such change and innovation have quite a limited impact on the culture and direction of a school or schooling overall. They allow the prevailing culture to incorporate the innovation so that it becomes part of what exists, rather than effecting change in the status quo. Caldwell (2005) and Beare (2001; 2003) create very strong pictures of the need for 'enterprise transformation' and the folly of not being strategic. The Specialist Schools Trust, a charitable, non-profit organisation funded by government and other sources, emerged in the UK to address this issue.

Specialist Schools Trust, UK

The Specialist Schools Trust works to give practical support to the transformation of secondary education in England by building and enabling a world-class network of innovative, high performing secondary schools in partnership with business and the wider community. The Trust was originally established in 1987 as the City Technology Colleges Trust to support the establishment of a number of Technology Colleges. In the 1990s the Trust expanded to include a wider range of specialist schools and is now at the heart of a network of over 2600 affiliated secondary schools, believed to be the largest network of schools in the world. The Specialist Schools Trust is the lead body for the Government's specialist schools programme. The Specialist Schools Programme helps schools to develop identities through their chosen specialities. The schools achieve this in partnership with private sector sponsors and through additional government funding.

<http://www.specialistschools.org.uk>

Of course, gradual change is the easy approach for schools and educators—keep what we have for the more academic student, ignore the reality that the world and how it creates and uses knowledge has altered, and maintain schools' focus on tertiary entrance results. This would retain the status quo, allowing selective schools and the traditional private schools to continue what they are doing. They are very good at it! I've said 'the easy approach', but in some ways it creates more stress because it asks teachers to change relatively small things often, thereby controlling teachers. How can teachers change and innovate if they are kept too busy and often stressed by constant peripheral curriculum and assessment changes? Further, gradual change has done very little to engage young people or combat the still terrible attrition statistics from schools, particularly those of young men and Indigenous young people.

Industrial era concerns and their effects

The reality is that our current system—that is, industrial era schooling—has not been concerned with education or learning, but with credentials and university entrance results. As a result, we now have up to one in five undergraduates dropping out within the first 12 months of starting university and two in five dropping out of the course they started and switching to something else. There is some evidence that only 40 per cent of those who leave university early ever go back. The statistics are hard to obtain because few universities are comfortable providing this information. The university attrition rate denies places to other young people and is a dreadful waste of human and monetary resources. It also is a damning indictment of the current system of tertiary entrance, based largely on school examination results. Clearly it does not work very well except as an expedient measure for the universities to select students. The failings of this system have been reinforced by a recent Monash University report (*The Age*, 7 April 2005) that shows that students from public schools perform better at university than other students despite lower tertiary entrance scores.

To maintain the status quo is also to continue to condemn many schools—public, private and Catholic—as failures because they do not rank well on the league table of high university entrance success. The status quo endorses selectivity and examination coaching. It does not respond to our knowledge of the modern world, its transformation, its labour market and what it really values. Moreover, it does not respond to the world of young people and their enormous talent for living and working in the 21st century.

On 30 May 2005, *The Age* featured the winning entries in its competition, 'The School I'd Like'. The senior student winner, Sophie Curzon-Siggers (Year 12, MacRobertson Girls' High School, Melbourne), expressed her frustration with the current education system. She advocated young people having the freedom to guide their own learning, addressing the power imbalances between staff and students, enabling students to set their own goals and expectations, redefining the teacher's role to one of guidance and students being able to decide the content and method of their learning.

A new emphasis

Schooling needs to model the workplace of the knowledge era. Schools must become part of the 21st century. There needs to be a life–work (the convergence of living and working) focus and an environment enabled by information and communication technology that is in touch with a global society. Therefore, schools must commit to working with the total person, not simply the academic person with some additional co-curricula and life-skills. Emotional intelligence, discussed in Chapter 4, should be at the core of schooling and the concept of self-management a key schooling outcome.

A number of Victorian primary schools have focused on developing programs to teach for emotional intelligence, including Laverton Plains Primary School.

Laverton Plains Primary School, Victoria

It was reported in *The Australian* that Laverton Plains Primary School in Melbourne's west has taken a multifaceted approach to developing emotional intelligence in its students. Children at the school explore their emotions and how to manage them, and learn about solving problems in relationships and dealing with conflict.

At the beginning of each term, each class from Prep to Year 6 learns about a different aspect of social interaction, including friendships, personal safety and dealing with bullying. In 2004, Year 1 at Laverton Plains learned about emotions through a program called Heart Masters. A new 'child'—a stuffed toy of the *Sesame Street* character Ernie—was introduced to the classroom, and the children learned how to make him feel welcome and included.

Discipline at the school is focused on restoring relationships rather than issuing punishments. The school is involved in a pilot program with the Catholic Education Office and the state Department of Education and Training to introduce 'restorative practices'. Students are encouraged to empathise with others and are involved in deciding what should be the consequences of any misbehaviour.

The Australian, 2 August 2004

Redefining knowledge

Schooling needs to review its whole understanding of the concept of knowledge.

Within an industrial society, knowledge came to mean academic subjects. Today, knowledge is the result of a process. Information is accessed and knowledge made from it, particularly usable, productive and commercial knowledge. We are also concerned with emotional and social knowledge.

Knowledge has become a process of development rather than being a developed product. In this era, information grows exponentially, so to try to confine it within 'knowledge'-based subjects is impossible. What is increasingly at stake is how we can access, make sense of and use information. This is process and the key to it is learning. In looking at traditional schooling outcomes, the work of Kerry J Kennedy (Australian National University, OECD, 2001: 205) proposes: 'Even those who attain well will need to be resilient and entrepreneurial.'

Convergence

A key word for the future will be 'convergence'. We will see the convergence of academic and vocational curricula. All students will be engaged in both curricula, developing the critical cognitive, emotional and social dispositions and skills for successful living and working. An additional element will be the pressure from the labour market for young people to engage in more work and work-based training as the effects of the decline in the population aged under 25 take hold. This work will be service, traditional trade and knowledge work, and with the last, fifteen-year-olds will be in increasing demand in areas such as Multimedia and IT.

An intention to change that focuses only on the traditional academic aspect will not bring about transformation. Schools would simply look at enhancing the methods in one particular area and the underlying issues would be overlooked or dealt with in traditional and generally unsuccessful ways. The discipline/anti-social behaviour issue is a major case in point. Pushing young people who are disaffected by schooling to do better academically will only increase their disaffection. Australian studies (Rowe, 2000) point to the problems of simply looking at curriculum change without considering the relationships between the problems and the culture, particularly classroom culture.

Fostering innovation

Schools must play a leadership role in developing the innovation and creativity needed for Australia to play any significant and competitive role in the global knowledge economy. However, schools are not currently equipped to assume this role because they are premised on an industrial paradigm of control of the curriculum, learning, assessment and credentialing, all of which are based on a very traditional view of what constitutes knowledge—predominantly traditional subject disciplines. Except in a small percentage of schools, few students are exposed to environments that foster their individual talents or empower their creativity through risk-taking.

Schools can only provide innovative learning and foster creativity when their environment allows risk-taking and individual and group exploration of learning. This is a leap in perceptions and expectations of schooling and often only occurs in settings such as outdoor education.

Really substantial cases of schools where creativity and innovative learning are fostered by an environment that allows risk-taking and individual and group exploration seem almost non-existent.

However, there is much evidence that suggests we believe that outdoor education can provide this experience. The Victorian Outdoor Education Association says: 'Students require direct experiences not abstract concepts ... OE is primarily experiential' (<http://www.voea.vic.edu.au>).

Many schools provide outdoor education, but there is little evidence that what they provide actually spills over to the culture and operations of the school proper. Even the many Year 9 off-campus programs do not have a direct relationship to the main campus program. Young people experience closer teacher relationships, independence, and some risk-taking during the off-campus programs, but are quickly reminded when they return to school that it is 'business as usual'.

If we can provide for such experiences in outdoor education and off-campus activity and we believe that they are valuable to developing young people, then we need to look at ways to provide real opportunities throughout their schooling for young people to grow. Simply providing short experiences without continuity does not create genuine or authentic learning. Outdoor education experiences need to be embedded in the schooling experience. However, central to providing such environments where young people can learn through risk-taking and exploration, is a culture that encourages teachers to model as risk-takers in their curriculum development and teaching.

Transformation at Eltham College

One way to illustrate the potential for changing teaching and learning is to look at what happened at Eltham College. In 2000, it set out to create an innovative change culture in a school that had always appreciated innovation, but had become settled into the grammar school-like, independent school tradition prevalent in Melbourne. The Eltham College Board and the new principal established an expectation of change, innovation and a total focus on students. A number of practical activities were developed as part of the change strategy to develop a more innovative and responsive school environment. A strategic directions vision paper was prepared and a five-year business plan was developed setting out the key long-term goals, core capabilities and strategies.

Vision was central and it needed a strong values context to validate how staff, students and the community would work together. These had to incorporate the networking and teaming of the new changing world.

It was important to introduce change quickly with high and articulated expectations for its success. Fast-paced change has to be legislated to make it happen; otherwise people 'muddle around' with it, try to avoid it or only partially work with it. To change attitudes and consequently behaviour, change needs to be enforced rather than trying to democratise schools through staff committees, consensus strategies and the like. These can come later in areas appropriate to teaching–learning, not through the strategic area that belongs to the Council and the chief executive officer. Clearly stakeholders, including staff, have to be consulted, but this has nothing to do with trying to arrive at consensus.

The key to staff change is the leadership and vision to create a 'working together' team. However, the team culture tends not to develop until after some of the shock of change recedes. Consequently at Eltham College, this whole early period of rapid, enforced change was very demanding on staff. In turn, however, staff wanted to be more involved in reviewing the changes and adding to them. Some of the major strategies we employed to bring about the change have been included on pages 85 to 87 of this chapter. The two most influential strategies were abolishing middle management, and giving students a voice through establishing strong expectations for change. Change activities also develop their own impetus over time and shape the culture of the school where people become accustomed to and anticipate change.

Eltham College did not engage in incremental, piecemeal or comfortable change. A culture now exists that expects change that is very much oriented to suit students, strategic directions and the environment. Staff now recognise that structures are transitory and will change to suit the environment and learning needs of students. Staff also recognise that changes are student-centred. Members of staff who do not want to be part of it either move on, or work with us to develop the skills needed to work effectively in the new environment.

While the school has come a long way towards creating the environment essential for the 'release and enhancement of individual student talent and the development of their creativity, freedom and innovation', it is still in transition. I suspect that schools should always be in a stage of transition—that is, in a change culture. Eltham College very clearly developed a strategy for communicating and consulting with parents, but was quite definite in moving beyond being customer responsive. The school was determined that it would continue to 'surprise and please' as a marketing strategy at the same time as listening to families. Parent consensus seems to be 'My son/daughter is happy, involved and learning, even if I am not sure that I like all the changes.'

Developing a knowledge era school involves change and we must recognise and acknowledge the discomfort that some people will experience, particularly teachers. We must have the stamina and belief to see through the changes and not stop part way. This has happened so much in Australian education and left us with very little real schooling transformation. Creating the culture for teachers to 'own their jobs' has helped develop an environment that models important attitudes and skills for young people.

Strategies for change at Eltham College

The major change strategies at Eltham College were:

- Sustaining strong visionary leadership that does not waver and that encompasses consensus.
- Using key strategies such as a single goal for the development of disposition and skill for self-direction across all curriculum areas.
- Giving greater ownership to students by upgrading the status of the student body and involving them in decision-making and collaboration.
- Establishing expectations that schooling is student-centred rather than teacher-centred.
- Having a very accessible and visible principal, particularly for students. This created some concerns for staff until they realised that we were focusing on a student-centred not a staff-centred school.
- Introducing a special program to develop positive ways of working together and establishing a culture of preventing anti-social behaviour that applied to staff and students.
- Changing the roles of executive staff to have across-school functional roles rather than simply being at the top of a triangle.
- Introducing a climate of freedom that encourages risk-taking by students and staff, where mistakes are viewed as a positive passage to learning. It should be put into the context of 'If it is supporting our vision, within our values context and we can afford it, do it!'
- Using student meetings or assemblies to establish positive expectations in students and staff. This is a very powerful measure. If the principal tells students what they can expect from the principal and teachers in terms of behaviour and relationships with students, then they tend to take it on board and expect that we will work with them.

- Creating a post-compulsory and, therefore, non-compulsory climate in the senior school that challenged traditional attitudes of teacher control. Senior school students need to be treated as young adults and have similar responsibilities and privileges as adults.
- Redeveloping the care system by removing the traditional pastoral care process and developing mentoring/coaching roles for those teachers who wanted to be carers, and helping young people to develop self-ownership of their own decisions and behaviours.
- Increasing funding both for professional development and to support individual and team innovation.
- Making the school, its curriculum, learning activities and processes transparent. Students, teachers and parents talk together: reports are to students and parents; interviews are three-way.
- Implementing a college Intranet curriculum, reporting and communication system with few hardcopy alternatives.
- Having very few written rules (except relating to safety/security); rather, working with people in terms of self-management and self-discipline.
- Modelling a working-together environment by the leadership.
- Creating individual ownership and the empowerment of individuals, staff and students by:
  - ¬ staff working as collaborative individuals within self-managing teams
  - ¬ abolishing middle management (heads of departments. Middle management positions were abolished and selective redundancies used.)
  - ¬ empowering students by establishing expectations for them to innovate and take risks. They know that it is all right to expect change and different teacher behaviours.
- Providing a strong investment in intellectual capital (staff) and introducing a performance development process for staff.
- Reducing lines of management and decision-making processes. The individual and the team should be able to make decisions and get on with their jobs. Teachers and their teams can own their jobs.
- Enabling opportunities that are important to student learning and success.
- Introducing vocational curriculum within the context of converging academic and vocational subjects, enabling all students to benefit from vocational studies. Valuing vocational alongside academic learning challenged existing thinking about the traditional curriculum.
- Allowing variation in uniform and how it was worn and permitting such things as age-appropriate jewellery and make-up, hats and hairstyles within the context of 'we look beyond the uniform to the individual'.
- Ending traditional forms of student punishment—for example the traditional Friday and Saturday detentions—expecting that, except if a major issue arose, teachers should deal with their own issues and assume responsibility for the whole student.

- Changing the established hierarchical order by inviting appropriate staff to be involved, not simply the normal power brokers on staff.
- Using a school-based enterprise agreement process to give greater professional recognition at the same time as establishing commitment to the college's strategic directions.
- Enhancing communication processes both internally and externally to the parent body. Regular media such as newsletters were improved, regular family letters were established, regular coffee afternoons were held to coincide with student pick-up times and regular parent forums were held at night.

New school culture, new focus

In supporting this culture of change, the knowledge era school must provide teachers with the right types of professional learning. Focusing on professional development that supports the school's directions first and the individual's needs second gives the correct perspective and balance in appropriate staff development. Therefore, at Eltham College, greater concentration has been on teaming skills, innovative practices, and IT (based on the use of the school's knowledge network, the online secure reporting and curriculum process). The school believes that it employs great teachers, provides professional development relevant to knowledge era schooling and ensures that when teachers leave they are better skilled than when they came.

The staff restructuring required to flatten the college's hierarchy may challenge some staff and sections of the parent community. Change can create anxiety, and when it affects your children, it is only natural to question what effects it could have on their learning and, in Victoria, what effects it might have on their tertiary entrance scores.

The primary focus during this transition period was to establish an acceptance that developing the disposition and skills for self-direction was a key college goal. The concurrent structural goal was the removal of middle management heads of department positions and placing responsibility on teachers and teams to be self-directed. The professional development budget was increased threefold and the school started to invest heavily in teams and individuals.

A secondary focus was the introduction of a program to prevent bullying or anti-social behaviour and the appointment of a coordinator to work with staff and students. The program, PeaceBuilders®, is as much about changing the culture of the school as it is about focusing on anti-social behaviour. It was designed to establish the way in which we all would work together. Bullying was not prevalent at Eltham College but neither was it immune to it.

A third focus was setting up expectations with students that the school was about them. Through leadership behaviour, they were empowered to question, to believe that change was possible and to become involved. Examples include minor changes to uniform expectations, making sport in senior school non-compulsory and ending the practice of detentions.

A fourth focus was fostering greater opportunities for vocational studies, particularly in Years 10–12 (and now years 7–12). This challenged the existing reverence for academic learning. Converging academic and vocational learning challenged traditional notions of intelligence, the value of academic subjects and their teachers, and the role of schooling.

The experience at Traralgon Secondary College

Other schools have used much more inclusive approaches to setting the change agenda. Change can be fostered in different ways. Traralgon Secondary College in Victoria used a community strategic planning approach to create a new, shared vision for the future.

Traralgon Secondary College, Victoria

In 2003, Traralgon Secondary College undertook a commitment to rethink the way in which it planned and carried out its work. Despite some successful individual initiatives in leading change and practice, the college had not linked this work with any aspect of its charter. A leadership team consulted with staff and students to imagine the future, identifying how students would learn in the future and how their school and classrooms should be designed. The team analysed and synthesised this knowledge to create a strategic plan, which identified a vision and set aims for student achievement, developed mission statements for curriculum provision, goals, targets and action plans, and identified projects, teams, resource and professional development opportunities.

Imaging the future—building the vision, Karen Cain, Principal, Lowanna College, 2005

Summary

Knowledge school era criterion 4: Modelling the 21st century in schools

Criterion 4 synopsis: The 21st-century school recognises the multiplicity of talents that young people bring to schooling and it commits to releasing and enhancing these talents. School creates opportunities for all young people. A significant part of the process of creating this is when the school and its teachers model the key attitudes and skills associated with living and working in the 21st-century knowledge era.

This chapter has explored the important criterion that shows that knowledge era schooling needs to be part of and model the real world of the 21st century. The table on page 89 provides a summary.

Knowledge era schooling	Industrial schooling
Models the 21st century	Models the 19th and 20th centuries
¬ is part of the real world	¬ is divorced from the real world
¬ teaches to manage life–work	¬ teaches subjects towards traditional careers
¬ develops multiple intelligences	¬ focuses on academic intelligence
¬ develops EQ and IQ	¬ focuses on academic intelligence/IQ
¬ converges the curriculum (academic and vocational)	¬ separates academic and vocational pathways
¬ focuses on student learning	¬ focuses on subject learning
¬ encourages self-management	¬ manages students
¬ is customised to the individual	¬ assumes 'one size fits all'

9 | The classroom and teaching

Teachers learn to work with young people, recognising their talents and skills and using their teacher skills and experiences to form a genuine collaborative learning partnership.

This chapter continues to address the fourth knowledge era criterion, 'Modelling for the 21st century', by looking at what all this means for teaching and the classroom. After all, teachers and classrooms have been around for a long time.

Teaching in a knowledge era school culture supports the teacher's role as an active participant in the learning process. Theorists (Berk and Winsler, 1995; Edwards, Gandini and Forman, 1998) from education, psychology and philosophy have identified the importance of human and social interaction. Vygotsky's concept of working within the Zone of Proximinal Development (ZPD) highlights the importance of the knowledge era teacher sharing an authentic warmth and responsiveness with the young person's learning.

Scaffolding, a notion associated with Vygotskyian theory, highlights the complex and delicately choreographed dance between the student and the teacher. The teacher is highly sensitive to the student's abilities and potential, always identifying times when it is necessary to lead the dance, to follow, or to dance alongside the student. The dance is never static, nor the same, but rather a constant creative process of reflection and modification. The notion of the dance is clearly analogous to developing the disposition and skill for self-directed learning.

Traditional classroom teaching

Traditional classroom teaching represents a simple equation for schools: four walls, twenty to thirty young people, one teacher and a timetable. Lessons progressed from introduction, homework check and lesson goals, new content, student activity and review through questions, to a quick sum-up and homework—with a bell as a full stop. For bureaucrats (and economists), this has been the cheapest way to offer mass education and the most effective method to manage students. Teachers needed skills in planning (long-term and lesson), group management, explaining, questioning, lecturing, providing some variety and setting student activities, assessing, preparing students for assessment, and report writing. The most important skill became classroom management: being able to control a group and having its members work, or at least behave. If teachers could manage young people through to the end of compulsory schooling, the disruptive non-learners would then leave and then teachers could focus on the subject and getting students successfully through the final year examinations.

The primary school classroom was slightly different, mainly because one teacher had the same class for most of the time. Hence, there was more emphasis on the students. Teachers got to know students and were able to plan for the individual. However, the routines associated with timetables, class management and assessing remained very similar, and there was never any doubt that teachers had the authority and the knowledge.

Beyond traditional teaching

Given the world of the global knowledge economy, the new knowledge era and the enabling powers of information and communication technology, the attitudes and skills currently being taught in schools are not enough to help 'Angelica explore her new world and develop her world view'. Indeed, they are not enough to help today's 15-year-olds move effectively through senior schooling to post-school success—witness the university and TAFE attrition rates.

As parents, we need to ask: What new approaches and skills are being developed so that schools and teachers can work better with our young people with their different attitudes, skills and access to information? We need to move beyond the belief that the school should undertake roles that are becoming increasingly difficult for parents to assume, particularly as our children get older. Schools should not be seen as the last bastions of a controlled, disciplined society. Even people in the military say that traditional mindless obedience is no longer useful or appropriate. Australia, for example, had pilots in the recent war with Iraq who refused to release their missiles because the intelligence they had been given seemed faulty when they reached their targets. Why would we want our schools and teachers to expect that young people should be different? We want young people to be self-disciplined enough to make conscious, appropriate choices.

Our young people rarely sit with their parents without having an opinion, without being able to converse about current events and without having the capacity to articulate an attitude about a given topic. Why should they behave differently at school? Certainly, we hope that they stop and listen to other people. We probably often reinforce this message at home. They learn that it may not be appropriate to state their views at particular times or in particular places, but we obviously do not want them to blindly assimilate others' opinions.

Sometimes young people just want to sit and reflect or do their own thing. At other times—and it's particularly the case with boys—they need to be active: they cannot sit still and the house seems too small for them. Yet, we have held the belief that young people will sit for up to six hours a day in a small, four-walled classroom, paying attention and confining their physical activity to recess and lunchtime. This applies not only to young men but also young women, who also want (indeed need) space and freedom.

Young people's need for space and freedom—which has always been a bane for parents—has not been catered for by traditional classroom arrangements. Compounding that, we now have young people's Internet and technology needs, the contrast between the stimulation from multimedia and TV and the general lack of stimulation in the classroom, and their need for constant communication shown in their simultaneous use of SMS text messaging while multi-tasking. Their honed skills and continual access to information leads to such reactions as, 'Hey teacher, I know that!' Or worse, 'Hey teacher, let's do something interesting. I can find that out on the Internet. Let's talk about how we can use it to … '

> It's all right … school. It's just if it wasn't so boring and strict, and they made it a little bit more fun, the teachers relaxed a little bit more.
>
> Slade, 2001

Teaching in the knowledge era

Knowledge era schooling involves better teaching and more interesting and challenging learning spaces or classrooms for all young people. We have reached a stage where even the 'traditionally bright' are insufficiently challenged to become what some call the 'know-how' intelligentsia. Knowledge era schooling means creating schools that young people enjoy and where they engage fully in their own learning.

I come back to the need to make learning enjoyable because without some fun, developing a good disposition towards being a successful learner generally does not happen. I suspect it is only people who have trouble having fun themselves that come up with 'School isn't meant to be fun. It is a serious place.' I don't know any school curriculum that can't be made enjoyable so that students can engage in it. We always need to be aware of the reactionary rationalisation about quality and standards. There are standards in the knowledge era schooling experience and outcomes that are so much higher than those we traditionally associate with academic standards assessed through external examinations. The knowledge era school builds quality and standards in through its attention to the notion of customising, to account for the multiple intelligences of young people and the convergence of EQ and IQ.

Primary school teacher education has had, for a long time, a student-centred approach. The young person in the classroom has been at the centre. Secondary education and beyond have focused on the subject (or discipline) rather than the student. Classroom teaching was devoted to imparting the knowledge and skills of the subject. We talked about individualising instruction, but in large classes that meant the top, the middle and the bottom ability levels, focusing most attention on the middle because it was the largest of the three groups. To achieve this, the class had to be well managed. This task was made more difficult by having to have the lesson finished within a narrow time frame, so students could get to the next class.

The knowledge era classroom

Four things are needed for the knowledge era classroom and its young people:

- adaptable space for people to move around in
- more flexible time rather than the restrictions of a tight timetable
- access to the Internet
- teachers who can collaborate with and engage young people rather than simply manage them.

Space

Providing space is more difficult and more demanding on resources than traditional classrooms. Twenty years ago we had open classrooms, particularly in the primary and early secondary years. They provided flexible space and much more room. However, we did not have the teacher skills in collaborating and structuring learning experiences and many school leaders saw them as poor examples of student management. They became associated with a laissez-faire attitude to teaching and learning. So, the open classroom was closed in again.

We know so much more today about young people and structuring learning experiences for them. We better understand boys and we recognise the powerful influences of information and communication technology. We are starting to recognise the importance of learning outcomes from a more integrated curriculum. We could use those open classrooms so much better today, but we don't have them. It is unlikely that governments will provide the resources to build new ones or even radically change old ones. Governments have rarely made education a top priority for spending and certainly have shown no inclination to invest in education. However, we can make some changes to old classrooms and school facilities.

Many schools are lucky in that they have some buildings that can be modified easily and quickly. Generally, however, most are built with lots of standard classrooms. So making physical alterations up front is not a strong possibility in bringing about change. I remember doing it many years ago at a school in Orange, NSW, where David Loader, past principal of MLC and Wesley College, and I converted the 'assembly hall' over the summer period into a large open space with carpets, portable dividers and so on as a change strategy directed at some well-established teachers. It worked. Teachers began to change their behaviours and how they structured learning experiences for students.

Using the physical space that is available can be a factor in teachers wanting to do things differently and being prepared to take risks. Part of it also is their being prepared to collaborate with colleagues as well as students. It is about attitude. The recognition that using physical space to support learning rather than to enclose it can have a significant influence on effective learning.

Eltham College uses its space to support effective learning. A walk around the Years 7–8 cluster areas will show some students in class working with a teacher, some in the cluster common room working as a small group, some in one of the IT areas and some in the library. The major thing you will notice is that they will be engaged in their learning and generally working as a team. On another occasion you will see some students in a science lab with a teacher, others outside building science experiments or models and others in a senior science lab working with a lab technician or senior students. If you look closely, you might also see some Year 3–4 students who have come down to check something out with a science teacher. In fact, their learning spaces align space, time and collaboration.

You won't hear any bells. Teachers and students manage their time.

Young people respect each other much more when they have some space and time and a culture that rewards working together.

Designing space

At Eltham College, our Year 9 team and senior staff prepared a scenario brief for Clarke Hopkins & Clarke Architects of Melbourne. The brief follows and the resulting design is on page 97.

CLARKE HOPKINS & CLARKE ARCHITECTS
Eltham College Year 9 Centre
Interpretation of Oral Briefing
July 2001

1.0 PART OF A DAY IN THE LIFE OF ELTHAM COLLEGE 'BUSH CAMPUS'
Written by Aine Maher

It's 8:30 a.m. and already students are arriving at the campus. A few have been here since much earlier; they have been involved in monitoring the movements and behaviour of a red-bellied warbler. This bird has interesting mating calls, but you have to be early to catch him! They have been fortunate and have taped the calls, as well as captured the bird and its movements on video. They remove gumboots and head towards the kitchen area for a hot cuppa and some toast.

One group of students is preparing for a morning in the lab. Their study of water requires them to analyse a variety of samples collected around the area. Their tests have focused initially on the chemical pollutants present in the water samples, but today they will be looking for those indicator organisms which tell about the overall 'health' of the water system. A visitor from La Trobe University will assist them in their recognition of the different organisms. Mr Mac is in the lab, setting up the video-microscope. They help him to organise the equipment needed as well as retrieving their results from previous pracs. Part of this activity is involvement in the Global Water Watch program. Students from 39 different countries are participating in this program where standardised tests are performed, and the results entered into a global database. These results can be analysed for global trends by all of the participating students. Some online friendships have started to emerge with students in Canada and Nigeria.

CLARKE HOPKINS & CLARKE ARCHITECTS
Eltham College Year 9 Centre
Interpretation of Oral Briefing
July 2001

Another group has been working together on a large mural. They have extracted pigments from a number of natural sources to complete the mural with an 'authentic' bush feel. It is quite large, and much negotiation has occurred within the group regarding the design. They hope to present the mural for the ECCA Master Artworks later in 2002.

The Hospitality Centre beckons for another group. As part of their LOTE program, they are exploring the cuisine of Indonesia. Satays and gado gado will be on the menu for lunch!

Yet another group is working on maths skills. They are looking at 'Estimation'. Just how do you 'guesstimate' the number of plants, or the number of ants, in a quadrant? Their new-found skills will also be useful for their session with Sarah from La Trobe later in the morning as recognition of organisms is not enough, you also have to know how many there are in a sample.

It's recess time, but there isn't much movement. A number of students choose to make a hot drink, and some head outside to shoot a few baskets. Others sit and plan a presentation they are giving to the whole group tomorrow. They are using PowerPoint, via the electronic whiteboard, and they have been delighted to capture the red-bellied warbler earlier this morning. One of them has found an enthusiast via the Web, and there are some marvellous photographs, which can be downloaded as part of their presentation.

Others are trying to set up a visit to an environmental reserve in Blackburn where there is quite often an extensive lake system. They have heard that the visitors' program there is worth seeing, and that there are some good ideas about presenting information in a novel way. If they are successful, that might be a worthwhile excursion.

There is much mirth in another area. One of the Webcams in the City Campus has caught the attention of some city-based friends. They are putting on a show for the benefit of their friends out bush.

A large group is gathered around the notice board where the electives for the following week have been posted. The 'tech' kids are delighted to see that the Solar Car project is on the list. One of them had done the initial research, and found a company to sponsor the purchase of materials. This will be a major project, occupying a deal of 'out of school' time. The local historical society is offering the opportunity for a group of students to work at the Andrew Ross Museum in Kangaroo Ground where archiving of collected materials is the major focus. For those who like history with a personal context, another group will be working with the residents of the Judge Bock home, spending time listening to them and collecting their personal histories. Yet another group will have the opportunity to work with staff at the Nilumbik Shire Planning Authority. They will be reviewing planning permission sought for developments in environmentally sensitive areas.

There is a reminder about the next deadline for the Community Service component of the Duke of Edinburgh Award scheme, with a list of possible activities for those who have not already started.

Groups 'swap' over the second session of the day. The mural is almost completed, and it makes way for the 'painting on tiles' activity where students use the symbols of the Aborigines to represent elements of the Eltham College environment. Seeing it through these 'eyes' creates a different understanding for them.

During the afternoon, all of the students hear a speech by Amy Nguyen. Amy's parents came to Australia as boat people. In spite of the odds, they have had enormous success through sheer hard work and unfailing optimism. Their dry-cleaning business is successful and Amy and her brother have enjoyed the benefits of a good education. Amy has been on a 'pilgrimage' to Vietnam to discover her roots. This has been a profound experience for her. Listening to Amy this afternoon is part of their work on Citizenship. They are exploring the reasons why people leave their homeland and the challenges they face as strangers in another world. How welcoming was Australia to the

---

CLARKE HOPKINS & CLARKE ARCHITECTS

Eltham College Year 9 Centre
Interpretation of Oral Briefing
July 2001

Nguyens? Has it answered their dreams? What expectations would they have of another country in similar circumstances? Did their parents, or grandparents migrate? Much discussion is generated by Amy's presentation. Students swap stories. Ms Mitchell asks them to think about ways in which they might present their responses to the ideas raised. Their creative writing task has a number of criteria that must be followed, but each knows the score by now.

The day finishes. Some students rush off to make it in time for the Intermediate band rehearsal at 4 p.m. Others want to follow up some references in the Eltham Library. The students who are presenting to the whole group are still working on their PowerPoint. They have managed to 'loop' the song of the red-bellied warbler and are delighted by the effect.

A notice on the electronic whiteboard reminds the students that they are away to Loyola tomorrow afternoon for ACS sport. In the morning, there will be DEAR (Drop Everything and Read), and Languages. Teachers will be available for consultation, and that big assessment task is due on Friday!

I was at a seminar recently with Karen Cain, former Principal of Traralgon Secondary College. As part of her talk (see Chapter 8) she described how their community planning process had identified the sorts of things that were needed in a 21st-century classroom. She showed us a PowerPoint presentation and I thought it was actually the classroom space side of our design. It wasn't. Different architects had come up with the designs from probably very similar briefs. Karen's classroom is almost the exact replica of the right-hand side of the design on page 97.

We do know what is needed for 21st-century learning space. Traralgon Secondary College and Eltham College each identified the same need for 21st-century learning spaces. We now need to commit the resources both to new learning spaces and to refurbishing the old ones.

Time

Time has always been over-controlled in schools, particularly in secondary schools. This is largely because we teach a multitude of subjects to large numbers of young people and also have reasonably large workforces of teachers. Traditionally, it has all been managed through a timetable where the two principle issues for secondary schools are the importance of the subject and the teacher-directed nature of curriculum and schools. Schools therefore control learning through allocating periods of time to subjects. When time is less an issue, learning engagement and schooling enjoyment are attainable.

Have you ever been in a modern workplace where workers are totally focused and on task for long periods without taking a break? The answer may be 'Yes', but not often. Generally, it is 'Yes' when people are so totally engrossed that time means nothing. Imagine how unproductive the modern workforce would be if it still worked to the Taylorist factory 'time whistles'. However, schools do! Why

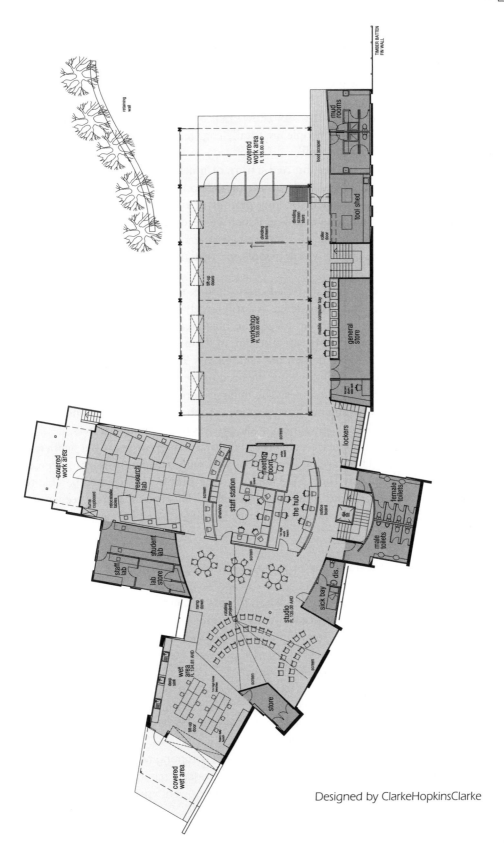

Designed by ClarkeHopkinsClarke

would you allow yourself to become totally engrossed in a project knowing that a bell will imminently force you to break away? I wonder how many senior students miss a class not because they don't care or have something better to do but because they don't want to interrupt the work they are doing in a free period? We can be sceptical, but how many of us really know? Our experience, however, tells us that it is wonderful when young people are totally engaged with their topic, when they can keep going without the 'bell'.

Because of the teacher-directed nature of much secondary schooling, most teachers prefer managed and limited time periods on the presumption that young people cannot listen or watch for long periods of time. When schools focus on engaging students, then time is less an issue. We need to see a shift from both the importance of the subject and the importance of teacher direction if we are going to create the time to engage young people, particularly those in the middle years (Years 5–9).

While we recognise state-based curriculum in terms of setting learning outcomes rather than content knowledge, we still largely organise our schools around separate subjects. We talk about integration but rarely do we practise it. We tend to assume that the senior years can take care of themselves. If universities demand traditional industrial subjects then the senior years are time enough to develop a subject discipline base. Until this time, we need to see learning in terms of learning process, engagement and outcomes. The middle years are when we alienate many young people from learning but if we provide the time and space, we would have a much better chance of engaging them in the process of becoming learners.

Young people and their teachers need the time to explore in greater depth and at their own pace. The learning process coupled with learning-to-learn outcomes should not be limited by time. Like adults, young people also need to be able to step back, take a break and sometimes just reflect. This is increasingly recognised in Melbourne with the city becoming a large learning space for Year 9 students in particular.

Giving time and space to the 'engagement risk' middle years is gaining emphasis in Victorian schools with a development of specific programs in Melbourne's CBD targeting Years 8–10 students. In addition to Eltham's City Campus in Finders Lane, which provides Year 9 students with two terms to explore the city environment, select issues for in-depth study, explore the relationship between school and work, and gain a better understanding of themselves and their ambitions, Melbourne's centre is gaining popularity as a giant classroom for thousands of students across the state.

More than 3500 students from 52 state schools will use the Education Foundation's City Centre in 2005. The one-week experience is aimed at helping students to think and learn in new ways and to build confidence. Students explore the city sights, undertake a research project and hear inspirational speakers.

City Cite, established by Ballarat Grammar and occupying two floors of an office building in Swanston Street is used mainly by independent schools and caters for up to 100 students at a time. Students experience the different aspects of a metropolis including the stark social contrasts between the retail luxury of Collins Street and the plight of the homeless sleeping on its streets.

The Herald Sun, 'Learn', 29 March 2005

However, care does need to be taken that the learning from such experiences is not tarnished by not recognising it as important to the culture of the rest of their schooling. If they come back and teachers tell them, 'You are now back into the real world of learning', then there will be no internalisation of the disposition and skill for self-direction.

Schools also can be much more creative with timetabling as Cramlington High in the UK shows.

Cramlington Community High School, UK

With its 'success for all' culture, Cramlington also is a good illustration of a transformed school and one that has turned to the further pursuit of schooling for the 21st century. It manages time for learning rather than allowing time to be the manager. It has systematic accelerated learning throughout its 1600 student 13–18 school. The traditional timetable is collapsed across the school for eight weeks to allow for intensive study and cross-curricular investigations and immersion. 20% of the senior curriculum is learned through independent learning. It believes in its students and their capacity to make judgments and succeed. Cramlington also knows about space and has built into the school common areas for students to chill-out.

<http://www.cchsonline.co.uk/>

The use of project learning can provide time for authentic learning. However, Professor David Hargreaves (2005) argues that major project work seems to be busy work and does not help young people learn to learn. He suggests ten criteria for good project work: the task is authentic; is co-constructed with teachers and students; has a clear worthwhile outcome; challenges and develops competencies; takes time; involves team work; involves seeking adult advice; engages students out of school as well as in school; provides students with a high level of feedback; and the completion of the project is openly celebrated. Bringing together the activity of project work, time, freer use of space and integrated studies (subjects) can make a difference to learning engagement. It also is one of the few things that individual teachers can do even if their colleagues aren't very interested in change.

Access to information

The third essential component of knowledge era schooling is access to the Internet. Access to the Internet does not mean computers in the classroom. It means recognising that young people today form the Internet generation. Let's remind ourselves of some of the statistics.

In 2002–03 (ABS, 2004) for those young people who accessed the Internet, it is estimated that:

1 341 600 (79%) accessed the Internet at home

1 181 900 (70%) accessed the Internet at school

412 400 (24%) accessed the Internet at someone else's home

117 000 (7%) accessed the Internet at a public library

57 200 (3%) accessed the Internet at other places (for example, Internet cafés).

Use of the Internet varied across the age groups:

For 5–8-year-olds, popular uses of the Internet at home were to play games (68% or 204 200), school or educational tasks (65% or 194 600), browsing for leisure (24% or 71 200), and using email or chat rooms (23% or 68 500)

For 9–11-year-olds, the Internet was used at home for school or educational tasks (89% or 409 000), playing games (60% or 275 300), using email or chat rooms (40% or 184 100), and browsing for leisure (39% or 181 100)

For 12–14-year-olds, popular uses of the Internet at home were for school or educational tasks (94% or 545 700), using email or chat rooms (67% or 390 700), playing games (52% or 300 200) and browsing for leisure (50% or 291 000)

Over half (61%) of the young people who accessed the Internet at home, did so more than once a week (824 800) and some (14% or 193 400) did so every day. The majority (70%) of young people who accessed the Internet at home every day were 12–14-year-olds, followed by 9–11-year-olds (23%) and 5–8-year-olds (7%).

The issue is not computers or laptops or having either of these in classrooms. It is the realisation that young people use the Internet often for their information and their learning. It is a significant part of their lives. The classroom needs to recognise this and ensure that the Internet is simply part and parcel of learning and students' convergence of living and working. This means today that home and parents also need to be part of the classroom.

The knowledge era school recognises that a fundamental change in the learning environment is required in order to prepare its students for a new working environment. Rather than emphasising the importance of hardware (which quickly becomes obsolete) the knowledge era school invests in creating easy access to information, for groups and the individual, through an online program that supports learning in an open and collaborative environment.

The Knowledge Network

An example of creating this environment at Eltham College was the development and introduction of the Knowledge Network with Corskill Australia, with the support of the National Office for the Information Economy (NOIE) (now the Australian Government Information Management Office).

The Knowledge Network has allowed:

- Students easy access to information as part of their education including:
  - ¬ individual study profiles and access to subject information
  - ¬ personal development reports
  - ¬ email access to their teachers.
- Teachers have direct links to:
  - ¬ class groups and individual students
  - ¬ parents
  - ¬ coursework and can provide continuous student online reporting and assessment.
- Parents can view their child's progress with daily access to:
  - ¬ curriculum content
  - ¬ assessment reports
  - ¬ email access to teachers and school administration.

The network was a core infrastructure upgrade in Eltham College's commitment to knowledge era schooling, which over the past two years has seen the school:

- create open and collaborative learning environments
- install multimedia technology designed for group learning, including Smart Boards, DVD players, sound systems, data projectors, and online access
- work with teachers to recognise the skills that students possess and use those strengths to encourage independent self-learning and network-learning skills.

The initiative is a copybook example of integrating information technology into Australian society, a high priority for the former NOIE, a government-appointed body responsible for overseeing the development of a national IT agenda for the education and benefit of all Australians. It recognised that one of the significant contributions the Knowledge Network can make is to motivate the greater community to start using information and communications technology, including parents who may have limited online experience.

Collaborating

Eltham College restructured its student organisation to better reflect the stages of learning, so it now has: Early Learning and Prep as a section; Years 1–4 as a section (Junior Years); Years 5–8 as a section (middle years); Year 9 as a stand-alone section; and Years 10–12 as a section (senior years). However, they all belong to the same school environment and culture, without any section assuming greater importance or status.

Teams of teachers, dedicated to a particular section, work collaboratively to design learning experiences. Eltham College has made a very clear decision that teachers, as far as is practicable, will work with a particular student section rather than teach across year levels. This is challenging in secondary because many teachers' career goal is to teach their particular subject to senior students. However, the college has generally removed the 'running' between a Year 7 class and a Year 12 class and asked teachers to focus their thinking, planning and energies on one particular student section that has been formed to suit where the 'kids are at', not where the teachers want to be. Importantly, this allows everyone to celebrate learning annually at each sectional level.

Eltham College no longer has a whole-school celebration (speech nights, final nights, etc.), but rather celebrations within each section. Often these occur more than once in any year, but with each section having a major celebration towards the end of the year. Eltham College wanted young people to feel great about their learning, not simply focusing on the next step, particularly the final year. These celebrations create a sense of fun and develop a love of schooling. Young people are encouraged to involve their parents in their celebrations and many of the activities. It is important for parents to love schooling too!

At Eltham College, students in Years 7–8, for example, have been arranged in clusters. The cluster mainly shares common and dedicated teachers, and members of the cluster share a staff office. They also are student mentors (care tutors). These teachers plan the curriculum framework for the classes in the cluster. They work towards common outcomes. Teachers and students can rearrange themselves to suit the particular activity. Sometimes, the cluster designs a 'Project Week'. Normal timetable is abandoned for this week and the students work collaboratively in small groups to investigate a variety of topics.

Students in Year 8 have tackled *The Rime of the Ancient Mariner*. They worked to understand the play, and the language and metaphor used in writing of that time. They wrote a script together, cast it, rehearsed it, staged it and presented it all within the space of a week.

Others investigated roller coasters, working from only rudimentary knowledge at the beginning of the week to developing large-scale models that were presented to a wide audience, complete with explanations about factors that were affecting their performance and design.

These experiences have been enormously enjoyable for the students, and enormously demanding of their teachers, but they are very powerful indeed. Here we have teams of learners, some younger, some older, all working together to create knowledge and understanding. Each operates as a self-managing team, and each has a weekly timetabled meeting and its own budget.

Teachers learn to work with young people, recognising their talents and skills and using their teacher skills and experiences to form a genuine collaborative learning partnership. Teachers model this in their teaching teams where, without the supervision of heads of departments, they manage their curriculum and budgets. Further, just as we expect with young people, teachers are in multiple teams.

Working together with young people concerns attitude and beliefs rather than skills. Skills of collaborating can be taught quite easily if the teacher has a positive attitude towards the notion of working with young people as opposed to managing and controlling them. The Board of the college also models this approach. Its annual strategic directions workshop is attended by four student leaders as equal participants and once each year the Board meets with the Student Council to deliberate on policy issues proposed by students.

For younger teachers the knowledge era is their world and the change to a collaborative style is therefore less difficult than for more experienced teachers. However, this is something of a generalisation and perhaps a little unfair on many experienced teachers. Once when I was showing some parents around our campus, an experienced and, indeed, our oldest teacher (64 years), who is a member of the Year 9 team, was asked, 'What do you teach?' Very quickly he replied, 'Kids.' He was then able to talk with them about how the Year 9 team, both in the city and in the 'bush', worked with their students. The parents expected an answer of Science or History or some other subject. However, John surprised them!

An important element is helping teachers towards a 'client/partner' relationship with their students. I use client to signify the student, particularly as they move through to their senior years, as the person who should be able to negotiate their learning programs. The student should feel that: 'As a client, I work with teachers to determine my learning needs and program rather than accepting what they think is best for me as part of a cohort of many other students.' This recognises that students have a role to play in setting their learning agenda. Teachers move from believing schools are about teaching to a belief that schools are about young people learning and learning to love it. Salter (2001) says it well:

> It's not about you; it's about them … Some teachers see themselves as the designated expert whose role is to impart their knowledge to students who are empty vessels. That's the wrong metaphor, says William Rando, who has been training college-level teachers for 15 years. The best instructors see themselves as guides. They share what they know, but they understand that they are not the focus. Their students are.

The knowledge era school's culture of working collaboratively, devoted to knowledge era skills and attitudes, has superseded the industrial era school's emphasis on 'doing to' young people. It acknowledges that the world view of young people is different from that of their parents and teachers. Values have not changed. It is the skills that young people possess that have changed—their learning styles have developed considerably and their changed access to information provides a broader and more complex view of the world.

Students and teachers have to learn to work together without the traditional domination of control and knowledge authority of the school and its teachers. Their skills are complementary: students can access a world of information far better than most of their teachers, but their teachers can guide them in its use, in creating knowledge from it and helping them to deal with the wide range of ethical questions that arise. The knowledge era school environment promotes easy access to information online and encourages students to collaborate with teachers to guide their own learning.

Knowledge era teaching skills

Teachers need to become important role models in this new classroom culture focused on knowledge era teaching–learning skills. The key skills for effective teaching in a knowledge era school include:

- collaboration and teaming
- shared leadership
- negotiation to arrive at shared expectations
- engagement management (managing learning rather than classrooms)
- creating and managing knowledge
- developing individual learning programs (customisation)
- self-awareness and self-evaluation
- self-management and self-directed learning.

These are far from being new skills. However, I am suggesting that they have become key teaching skills for the knowledge paradigm.

It is a quantum leap, involving our expectations, how hard we challenge young people and how we structure the learning experience. Our students must be able to learn effectively within the knowledge paradigm. They need to become knowledge workers. Such workers are people who must make informed individual decisions in order to be able to do their job, but who also recognise that they are part of a team or many teams. As parents we are becoming more aware that schools have to be more than university entrance factories (a good industrial metaphor). Recent newspaper articles direct attention to parents seeing that 'life-skills' and preparation for the new world of work are increasingly important to their perceptions of what constitutes a good school. One of our LifeWork Counsellors (in old terms, career counsellors), Sara Browne, wrote the following for staff and parents:

> Our young people need to become knowledge workers who will need to learn continuously for more than forty years. They will need knowledge of new employment-related expertise, new self-knowledge and new and predicted futures, which are the features of the changing employment landscape. Instead of the traditional view of career, it can now be defined as: 'The process managed by an individual that consists of all the varied experiences in education, training, work and occupational fields'. The person's own career choices and personal search for fulfilment are the unifying element.
>
> Children as young as four have developed very clear beliefs regarding work and its role within people's lives, and they continue to develop and refine these views throughout their school life. The more experience and knowledge we gain about ourselves and the society we live in, the more relevant and effective our decisions will be. The primary purpose of Career Development, therefore, becomes to provide opportunities for students to be successful and self-reliant in planning and managing their careers in a rapidly changing knowledge economy.

In order to develop and build upon this knowledge the area of careers requires a different approach within schools. No longer is it appropriate to wait until students are 14 or 15 to begin career education. Viewing career as a lifelong process, not as a structure will enable us to tap into and develop the career-related knowledge that our children are amassing. Integrating career education into the curriculum provides opportunities to give relevance to the work done in class, relating it to future life–work. Developing and implementing an intentional, whole school, integrated and developmental approach to career development becomes an important and integral step in meeting the needs of our young people.

If a significant part of what we as educators do is prepare our students for their lives after school, we need to give value to a life–work program. As such, we need to move beyond the narrow confines of 'career' to integrating LifeWork into our total curriculum.

Schools, in responding to the issue of life–work preparation, need to recognise that an important way to start this is to release the talents and the information-age skills of young people and use teaching skills to enhance them. We need to recognise that as teachers we are knowledge workers and should be modelling the life–work behaviours for our young people. Perhaps more than any other generation, young people today can call our bluff relatively easily and see through the 'do as I say not as I do' practices of the past. These are the 11- to 14-year-olds who are wise to the rhetoric of politicians about war, weapons of mass destruction, health policies, election promises and the like.

So, before teachers can develop knowledge era skills, they need new attitudes towards young people, their world, their developing world views and their modelling of knowledge work. As discussed, in knowledge era schooling the expectation that 'as a teacher I need to be respected, listened to and obeyed simply because I am a teacher and I am in a school' needs to be replaced. Rather, attitudes should reflect the following:

'I need to be respected and I will give you equal respect because I am a human being' is a much better start to developing younger people–older people working relationships.

'We need to learn to work together, but I probably will be a little more tolerant than you because I have more experience and maturity and so we can learn together' is a healthy way to think about the differences between younger and older people.

'As an older person I have a responsibility to help you learn the expected ways of society from ethical, legal and workplace safety perspectives, but I am not going to impose rules simply to make my life easier by controlling you' is a moral way of working through the issues associated with societal values and standards.

'As an older person, I need to learn from you, your new world and your developing world view as it is different from mine and because the world is so different, I am not going to impose my world view on you' is to respect young people and to make a significant step forward in closing the traditional sense of generational gaps.

Summary

The knowledge era classroom of the 21st century requires:

- adaptable space
- flexible time
- access to the Internet
- collaboration between teachers and young people
- teachers as important role models who focus on knowledge era teaching–learning skills.

A new learning environment culture needs to emerge.
The new skills will combine to develop a teacher with
very different capabilities for working with young
people and very different attitudes towards how young
people can engage with schooling.

Knowledge era schooling criterion 5:
Different learning and teaching skills:
self-management and self-directed learning

Knowledge era teaching and learning skills include: collaboration and teaming; sharing leadership; negotiating to arrive at shared expectations; engagement management (managing learning rather than classrooms); creating and managing knowledge; developing individual learning programs and customisation; innovation and creativity; risk-taking and entrepreneurialism; adaptability and managing complexity; teaching for self-awareness and self-evaluation; and teaching for self-management and self-directed learning.

Modelling the life–work world as teacher–knowledge workers is challenging because traditionally teachers have been taught to value security and a secure job for life. School leadership needs to take action to create the new world for teachers, unless of course we believe that this world and its labour market are just temporary and we will quickly return to corporate responsibility to provide jobs for life. There is no evidence that this will happen.

In creating an environment of knowledge workers at Eltham College, the school developed a situation in which teachers had to take ownership of their jobs and continue to demonstrate their effectiveness, their capacity to innovate, their willingness to team and their commitment to the school's vision for schooling for young people. Enterprise agreements, discussed in Chapter 7, are an important illustration. For the first time, these agreements gave teachers professional status where they accepted responsibility for their own jobs and Eltham College accepted responsibility to recognise them on merit and create the conditions in which they could thrive as creative educators.

Within this context teachers are part of a performance development program that allows them to own their own job as professionals. They negotiate their goals for the year within the context of the school's strategic directions, identify their own professional development needs in relation to this and demonstrate what they have achieved.

Apart from a few independent schools, teachers' pay and conditions are modelled on the public service under union awards—incremental steps for everyone with no rewards for being a professional. Until teachers can move away from a 'one hat fits all' model they will be regarded as second-class professionals. This is unfortunate because teachers do contribute to wealth creation, unlike many of the widely recognised professionals (such as doctors, accountants and solicitors who are service professionals).

Teachers should be developing innovative and entrepreneurial young people needed to create a vibrant, competitive and more equitable Australian economy within the context of the global knowledge economy. Unions need to change their approach to supporting teachers if they are to allow them into the faster-paced and higher-paid professions. Professor Hedley Beare (2002) outlines seven characteristics that would be required of a successful knowledge era school. He describes a key difference concerning the role of teachers and teacher unions. He predicts that teacher work styles will become radically professional, likening the teacher to an independent contractor. In relation to unions he talks about 'employee mutuals' that market, train and manage their members, rather than trying to negotiate set conditions for all. The latter does not take into account merit or job ownership. It maintains a low-level status quo.

So, in relation to teachers in the knowledge era school there are many issues to confront. The union issue will probably be the most difficult. However, there is still much that can be done to move towards an environment in which young people are given the best chance to become creative and risk-taking knowledge workers in the 21st century.

A new learning environment culture

What are the new skills associated with teaching and learning teachers will need to develop? A new learning environment culture needs to emerge. The new skills will combine to develop a teacher with very different capabilities for working with young people and very different attitudes towards how young people can engage with schooling. We can learn much from the theories and practices associated with early learning (Berk and Winsler, 1995).

Frequently, too much emphasis is placed on learning styles rather than recognising that while people may have a preferred style, as life-long learners we will have to learn in many ways, most often as self-directed learners, increasingly using e-learning opportunities. The Demos Working Group (2005) stated:

> Whilst is may be true that some learners have a dominant learning style, a good education does not limit them to that style or type, but ensures that students have opportunities to strengthen the other learning styles. Whereas bad professional practice restricts opportunities and narrows intellectual development, good practice uses these schemes as ways of expanding opportunities and widening ways of learning. In misguided hands, learning styles could become not a means of personalising learning, but a new version of general intelligence that slots learners into preconceived categories and puts unwarranted ceilings on their intellectual development and achievement.

The redefining and development of teaching skills is a key step. If we consider the Reggio Emilia educational approach (Edwards, Gandini and Forman, 1998) it is not difficult to draw upon the similarities to knowledge era schooling criteria. Indeed, it helps us understand that providing space, time, freedom to explore, having young people and teachers working collaboratively while sharing their intellectual and emotional intelligence, and constructing and co-constructing knowledge, are important for all young people from preschool to the final years of schooling.

Teaching skills in the knowledge era

Let's examine the knowledge era teaching skills introduced in Chapter 9 in more detail.

Collaboration and teaming

Collaboration and teaming means that teachers and students work together in a partnership of learning. This is not a new skill; many teachers use it frequently but generally discriminately and/or randomly. That is, they work well in partnership when they are at a camp, on a trip with a small group or even in class with a select group. Collaboration is a core skill to be used all the time with all students. Younger and older people can work together in planning activities that will involve students in achieving the learning outcomes being sought; for example at Eltham College, teachers and students plan together their project activities week (Years 7–8) or their medieval day (Year 8). In Years 5–6, teachers and their students work together with other teachers and community groups (such as the Nillumbik Reconciliation Council) to create annual reconciliation events and very public reconciliation murals.

As part of this process, teachers need to be able to recognise the influence of students as teachers and the opportunities they make for themselves. I continue to return to the story about young people and technology. Young people rarely turn to an adult for assistance; they work with each other, learn from and teach each other. Given young people's immersion in this new world, we need to be able to acknowledge their partnership in the learning environment and accept that they will teach their peers and teachers.

One of the large issues with the notion of students as teachers is how well teachers can accept the change of status from being the purveyors of knowledge, as has been their historical role, to one of sharing the learning environment. Eltham College's Years 3–4 teachers were able to illustrate their acceptance by opening up learning spaces for their students to teach their parents what they are learning and how they are learning it. There are nights where all parents come into the History Centre so that their children can teach them what they are doing: the young people and their teachers plan evenings so that parents work through the goldfields, do their maths and journal writing and engage in simulated experiences of life in Australia after the Europeans arrived.

Some of this can be found in the special experience programs that schools have set up for their Year 9 students in particular. Wesley's Year 9 one-term experience is an example of where young people are empowered to assume greater management of themselves in collaboration with their teachers.

Wesley College, Victoria

The aim of the Wesley College residential learning village project is the education of the whole person in a community. Wesley @Clunes provides students with an eight-week residential educational experience. Students live in houses with seven other students. Staff residences are located throughout the campus and staff are rostered on duty 24 hours a day to supervise students and run the educational program for the entire eight weeks. Students are responsible for all aspects of their domestic life while in residence, including shopping, cooking and cleaning. Living in this environment helps provide students with a greater understanding of what it means to become more adult and gain a truer understanding of their place in the world.

There are no bells or normal subjects, and the curriculum is negotiated between students and leaders in a collaborative manner. The Clunes program provides opportunities for students to take some control and responsibility for what they learn. In doing so, the traditional relationship between student and teacher has been reconstructed. A different focus has been given to the educational process, where the learning emphasis is more individualised, and one where the emphasis is upon personal relationships and community rather than just academic pursuits. Students are required to reflect on themselves as learners and examine ways to enhance the learning process.

<http://www.clunes.wesleycollege.net.>

Such projects provide valuable insights that we need to reflect on: How can these things happen where there are no Clunes-type opportunities? Why can't this happen in school?

Shared leadership

Shared leadership again involves working together on issues, policies, strategies and directions in and out of class. From a school perspective, for example, student leaders are directly involved in policy deliberations and reviewing critical issues. Students, without any formal position, such as Eltham College middle years students, who successfully sought a uniform change by taking it to a staff/parent/student uniform committee, need to feel that they can express their leadership and make a difference. Students and teachers need to be able to work together in planning learning activities, and use of time and space. Salter (2001) says:

> You're teaching people how to think. The last thing you want to do is stand up and tell people what to do. Or give them the answers that you want to hear. The best instructors are less interested in the answers than in the thinking behind them. What leaders have to offer is a 'teachable point of view', says Noel Tichy, a professor at the University of Michigan Business School and author of *The Leadership Engine: How Winning Companies Build Leaders at Every Level* (Harper Business, 1997). It's how they look at the world, interpret information, and think through problems. The best teaching leaders help people learn how to think on their own rather than telling them what to think.
>
> 'You want a forceful group of people who know what you want but at the same time feel free enough to make the day-to-day judgments themselves,' says Gene Roberts, a long-time editor at the *Philadelphia Inquirer* and the *New York Times* who now teaches journalism at the University of Maryland at College Park. (During his 18 years at the *Inquirer*, the paper won 17 Pulitzer Prizes.) 'You have to know when to let go so that people don't become dependent on you. In the newspaper business, speed is everything, and if you have people waiting to hear what you have to say before they will react, you'll get beat.'

Lipson Community College and Stoke Dameral Community College, UK

At Lipson Community College and Stoke Dameral Community College in England, teams of 13- to 18-year-olds are being taught how to teach their friends, teachers, parents and siblings about online dangers and how to stay safe. The Teenangels project, introduced from the United States, helps older students learn how to protect themselves and fellow students from the perils of cyber bullying, stalking and grooming, as well as identifying theft and being spied on online. It is based on the belief that teenagers are able to educate their peers on Internet safety more effectively than parents or teachers. The aim is for fully trained Teenangels to take their knowledge into primary schools in Plymouth to teach younger children. The program demonstrates a practical manifestation of student empowerment and student voice.

<http://www.lipson.plymouth.sch.uk/default.htm>

As with the Lipson and Stoke Dameral community colleges, young people need to believe that they will be heard and can make a difference through a school culture that is open to them and has formal school policies and processes for student voice.

Negotiation

Negotiating to arrive at shared expectations is an important skill for teachers and students to learn. So often, it is misunderstood to mean consulting or simply telling. Sometimes students even think they can negotiate after the event. It means that people who are seeking different outcomes from a common issue are prepared to work through their expectations of it and arrive at mutually agreeable outcomes. Not an easy task, but always achievable if the willingness is there.

The importance of negotiation in establishing expectations about how the group will work together and also how families can work together cannot be under-estimated. Both parties have expectations that need to be shared and understood, then they agree on common expectations and finally, come to agree on what is fair when expectations are not met. At Eltham College, for example, twelve months ago teachers expressed concern over the use of camera phones around the school by some students. Rather than calling for a ban and confiscations and so on, they took the issue to the Student Council to negotiate a revised mobile phone protocol to incorporate camera phones. Another approach to negotiated expectations can be seen in the following study from Failsworth School in the UK.

Failsworth School, UK

The Failsworth School in the UK had a positive discipline plan in place when designated a specialist sports college in September 2000. To capitalise on the ethos of sport and to use an analogy the students understand we decided to name the plan the Fair Play Plan.

To make the plan workable teachers were asked for the four things which they would like eliminated from the classroom.

Students were asked what they wanted and expected of a discipline system.

In essence the students demanded consistency when teachers applied rules and teachers wanted to eliminate low-level disruption. To this end we decided on Fair Play Rules. In sport students accept instant sanctions for unfair play.

<http://www.schoolsnetwork.org.uk>

Eltham College uses negotiation to arrive at shared expectations and consequences. The following is the document that teacher Cath and the young people in one of the Year 5/6 multi-age groups put together.

EVERYTHING STARTS WITH A CHOICE ...
NO EXCUSES ... NO BLAME!
THE CLASS AGREEMENT FOR 5/6 H 2005!

Together we have negotiated this agreement! Together we can make it work! We agree to do our best to abide by the expectations set out below. We will help and remind each other to meet these expectations.

SOLVE PROBLEMS FAIRLY
Own our own actions! Listen to each other! Hear all sides of the story! Be fair to all, not just your friends! Seek a wise person to help! Stay calm! Speak quietly! Sometimes we need to compromise! Talk face to face, not behind people's backs!

TAKE RESPONSIBILITY!
Tell your story honestly! Don't let someone take the blame! Don't take the blame unfairly! Think first! Speak respectfully! Apologise for hurting or offending! Act sorry; don't just say 'sorry!' Don't copy other people's behaviour! Think for yourself!

CARE FOR EACH OTHER
Actively include everyone! Be aware of other people! Move carefully, in classrooms and around corners! Cheer up people who feel sad! Make sure everyone is participating! Don't put people down! Respect people's feelings! Praise people!

WORK EFFECTIVELY BY OURSELVES AND WITH OTHERS
Talk quietly! Stay focused! Listen to all ideas! Contribute! Everyone shares the work! Have a positive attitude! Use time wisely! Let everyone have a fair go! Work with lots of different people! Do your best! Help others!

ACTIVE LISTENING!
Listen with your eyes! Don't interrupt, distract others or fiddle! Take part in the conversation or discussion! Put up your hand! Take turns to speak! Be respectful of people's suggestions! Make appropriate comments!

HAVE FUN TOGETHER!
Greet people and farewell them! Invite people to join you! Smile at people! Loosen up! Enjoy each other's company! Include everyone; don't leave anyone out! Make everyone feel important! Enjoy working together!

OUR TEACHER WILL BE
Happy and colourful! Fantastic, caring, enthusiastic and kind to us! Understanding! A friend! Appreciative of us! Someone who listens to our ideas! Someone to talk to if we're down! Helpful and positive in attitude! Patient and encouraging! Fair! Able to explain things clearly!

OUR CLASSROOM WILL BE
Friendly and peaceful! Cared for; neat and tidy! Full of happy people! A positive place! A great place to learn! Lively, joyful, exciting, and fun! Creative and interesting! An Argument Free Zone! Like one big family! A colourful environment! A PeaceBuilders Place!

Sign here!

I _____ **participated in designing this agreement and will do my best to behave according to the expectations outlined above.**

SIGNED:_____

DATE: ____/____/ 05

WHAT HAPPENS IF WE BEHAVE IN A WAY THAT DOESN'T RESPECT THE AGREEMENT?

Participating in class and school activities and events is a privilege. We know that we want Peace-Builders representing our class/school. Sometimes we forget what we should do or say and we make a mistake. Sometimes we do not act responsibly or with care for others. As PeaceBuilders we are expected to right wrongs. If we have behaved in ways that are not part of our class agreement or PeaceBuilders then we might:

- discuss the problem with other students, parents, teachers
- write about what happened
- apologise verbally
- apologise in writing
- be asked to work or play in another area
- be asked to do some research on the possible consequences of our behaviour
- be withdrawn from a class activity or event.

Sign here!

I _____ **accept the above consequences discussed by our 5/6H class.**

SIGNED:_____

DATE: ____/____/ 05

Engagement management

Traditionally teacher education programs for new and experienced teachers have focused on classroom management rather than emphasising engagement in learning and working together.

Engagement captures young people's belief in learning and their capacity to be effective learners. To engage is to create interest and have fun. Stoics will tell us that education is not about fun, but rather instilling the required learning in a disciplined fashion. However, research (ANTA, 1997; Warner, Christie and Choy, 1998) into self-directed learning showed that up to 70 per cent of the workforce and tertiary students had limited disposition and skill for self-directed learning. They did not have the personal belief that learning was important and worthwhile for them. One of the reasons is that learning at school has not been engaging. If we want life-long self-directed learners we have to help them believe in learning and themselves; we have to engage them as active participants. Active participants are young people who want to learn and are prepared to have fun doing it.

Too many people still believe that if a young person is having fun learning, then it must be too easy or it is not real learning. It is so easy for reactionary critics to try to take the debate down a 'school and learning standards' track focusing on traditional schooling outcomes. Eltham College's Year 3–4 young people would argue differently—and remember, this is a very important age for the core learning skills of literacy and numeracy.

Eltham College's history centre program

Students in Years 3 and 4 experience a fascinating insight into the early days of European settlement in Australia through their involvement in a dynamic history program. A dramatic simulation allows students and teachers to role-play; negotiating their way through realistic historical events of early pioneer and convict times, and confronting the problems created in daily pioneer life. By refurbishing a traditional classroom cluster area into the History Centre, Eltham College has created spectacular historical environments, such as the *Endeavour*, an early Sydney town and the goldfields. At other times it can be a pharaoh's tomb or even an emerging city.

The program promotes hands-on, independent learning and integrates the wider curriculum to include journal keeping, numeracy, music, art and Mandarin Chinese. Imagine being at the goldfields: you maintain contact through letter and journal with family back home, you have to work through your gold weights with the banker and determine how much you have earned, what you have to pay out, what goes home and what goes to your life on the diggings. Fun? Yes! Learning? Certainly! These young people do national testing in Years 3 and 5 and parents access results. Their results are good, so even in traditional terms, young people can converge fun and learning.

Learning to love learning is more than engagement in an activity in a timetabled lesson. It is about the bigger picture of being engaged in achieving the outcomes for the term, semester, year, and entire duration at school and beyond. Certainly, the lesson is a good start, but it needs to extend to a more open learning environment where young people have space and time to be themselves and, at the same, time engage with their teams in quality work as in the following case.

Buckley Park College, Victoria

At Buckley Park College, a focus on improved learning and teaching practices led to a comprehensive professional development program to expose teachers to leading experts in the subject. The new knowledge and capabilities of teachers drove the creation of special units of study. Several times during the year, the normal subject-based curriculum is suspended and students take part in a task-based learning unit that allows them to make connections between theoretical lessons in class and their application in life outside school.

<http://www.buckleyparkco.vic.edu.au>

As with so many good case examples, the illustration is about an extra initiative rather than being embedded into the culture of learning throughout the whole schooling experience.

Creating and managing knowledge

The knowledge era has seen an exponential growth in easy to access information and the new dominance of knowledge of the global economy. Schools have to move on from being purveyors of knowledge, traditional and subject-based. Vocational learning and academic learning need to converge and there needs to be much more applied learning where young people learn by doing. We cannot continue to create 'square pegs' when the holes are all different shapes! We can no longer regard schools as institutions that teach how to find information and impart 'bookish' subject knowledge to young people. In fact, teachers cannot keep up with the rate of changing information available. Look at the speed at which history is being rewritten and look particularly at how new discoveries are challenging established scientific beliefs.

Schooling has to ensure that young people can take their skills of accessing information and add analysis, problem solving and evaluation skills to create knowledge or at least understand the ways in which they can create knowledge. Creating knowledge does not come about by undertaking doctoral-type research, but rather by learning to think critically about information, making decisions about what to do with it and then using it.

The key is 'learning to apply'. Students need to be in learning situations where they can, and, indeed, have to learn through application. For the past 200 years our thinking about learning has been directed at the conceptual and cognitive levels. It has been discriminatory because some people relate quickly to abstract, conceptual levels while others do not. Traditionally, those who do not relate quickly to abstract concepts have been disadvantaged at school.

If we can better integrate the creation of knowledge, learning how to use information and making decisions about it, with practical application, then young people will be able to increase their disposition and skill to be knowledge creators throughout their lives. We need to see application as a pivotal point in young people becoming confident and successful learners. Maths can be applied as much as Multimedia and Hospitality.

Applying learning requires doing, not sitting, listening or taking notes. It involves active engagement. In Years 7 and 8, this engagement could include creating small teams and publishing a magazine, or researching and building mechanical toys or medieval siege instruments, or doing a certificate level course in Information Technology.

At Eltham College, Year 9 students use Maths, Science, English and Social Studies as part of a permaculture program to manage elements of the environmental reserve and to run their own coffee shop, which is open to the public. Years 1 and 2 direct their learning to 'greening' as in a sustained environment within a large breakout area or creating Greek cultural models. Senior students apply their subjects to working with the Year 1 students in film-making, converging Hospitality with Business and so on.

Smithfield High School in Queensland provides another strong illustration.

Smithfield High School, Queensland

The strong emphasis on information technology at Smithfield State High School sees over 70 per cent of students enrolled in at least one or two information and communications subjects. Successful business partnerships with Microsoft, Hewlett-Packard and NEC have assisted the school to identify parts of the curriculum that can be tailored to match IT industry skill shortages and therefore ensure that students are gaining relevant workplace skills. The school is now in demand from organisations wanting web site design services. One project has seen senior students linking PC tablets to global positioning navigation systems and digital cameras to create a virtual tour of the Cairns Botanical Gardens.

<http://www.smithfieldshs.qld.edu.au>

As with Smithfield, vocational learning, real life–work opportunities and networking with employers add significant reality to learning for young people to become life-long learners. It also helps all young people understand the life–work that is part of their lives. Young people who go on to university are engaged in vocational education and training and most have to find work during their university courses. Many young people are engaged in paid work from about 15 years old. Why not create a more seamless learning environment for them where they can experience schooling, post-schooling and employment as part of their 15–25 year age group experiences?

It is time we recognised the power of applied learning by ensuring that learning has time and space. Short class times with young people and their teachers locked within four walls do not offer opportunities for most young people to find their best.

Developing individual learning programs

It is time we committed the effort and resources to develop learning programs that are more tailored to individuals and their learning styles and needs. This does not mean individualising instruction in the classroom. We need to be able to assess early and at transition stages students' learning needs, capabilities and aspirations and help them plan for their ongoing learning experiences and personal outcomes.

Parents need to ask schools what they do to diagnose their children's talents and capabilities. Then they need to ask how schools are matching their learning programs with the individual young person.

For us in schools, this will mean that we need to continue to reconfigure schooling by acknowledging that learning does not reside in class groups in traditional classrooms; nor in class size and having smaller and smaller class groups; nor in having additional support teachers to provide programs for those with additional needs. Learning should be a total package where teachers, counsellors, learning support staff, librarians, IT people and so on are seen as teams focusing on developing and implementing the individual learning program for each young person.

Knowledge era schooling requires that we transform the way in which we see young people; we need to recognise their talents as individuals, and not identify them simply as class groups. When we talk about working together and in partnership, we need to recognise that these words describe individual relationships in a collaborative setting. While we continue to think in terms of the class group we will have a teacher as a position of authority rather than a teacher as an older, mature person guiding, facilitating and helping young people manage their learning.

Schools in the knowledge era need to customise learning at all stages of schooling. While it is easier in the senior years of school, it needs to be part of the process of schooling from the early years. I believe that this is an important element of scaffolding as discussed in Chapter 4.

The development of individual learning plans, a strong concept associated with customisation, is not new.

The Australian Science and Mathematics School in South Australia has the development of these plans between students and tutors as part of the normal operation of the school.

McGuire College in Victoria has developed the concept in relation to student pathways to senior schooling, further education and training and employment.

Australian Science and Mathematics School, SA

At the Australian Science and Mathematics School, tutors work with students to develop individual learning plans which are based on their strengths and interests, their immediate and long-term ambitions, and developing strategies for student success. These strategies may include helping students to meet assignment deadlines, to discover career preferences and pathways, and online learning tools to assess preferred learning styles. Greater engagement in individual learning plans occurs when students develop them as web-based portfolios which include their interests, skills and ambitions.

<http://www.asms.sa.edu.au>

McGuire College, Victoria __|

McGuire College is a co-educational secondary school of around 640 students located in the south of Shepparton in Victoria's north-east. At the end of the 2001 school year, 46% of Years 10–12 McGuire College students had individual pathway plans. The Managed Individual Pathways (MIPs) initiative facilitates the college goal of improving and enhancing student awareness of their options for further education, training and careers. To this end, the following initiatives have been implemented as part of the college's overall MIPs strategy:

- The compulsory Industry and Enterprise Unit in Year 10 includes the use of Guest Speakers, Workplace Visits and Videos, University Information Sessions, Careers Expos, and Career Recruitment Providers. Year 11 and 12 students are also exposed systematically to follow-up programs in these areas.
- Individual course counselling provided by trained staff for selected Year 10 and 11 students, using student academic performance and career prerequisites as a basis for discussion.
- Transition programs for students moving from Year 10 to 11, and Year 11 to 12.
- A web page for the College website is currently under construction to enable all students and their parents to access the latest information on matters relating to career planning and future options. This initiative will supplement the activities undertaken in Home Groups and the information distributed via newsletters. It will also reinforce the college's efforts to provide a framework that empowers students to engage in their own research and take ownership of their own futures.

<http://www.mceetya.edu.au/stepping/casestudies/rec20.htm>

Both case studies introduce notions of scaffolding, but I would argue that knowledge era schooling requires a much more strategic approach throughout schooling, and, therefore, essential links at each stage of the schooling journey.

Self-awareness and self-assessment

Self-awareness and self-assessment are critical elements in teaching for emotional intelligence. Goleman (2004) argues that 'It is fortunate ... that emotional intelligence can be learned.' While he goes on to say that it is not easy, we also recognise that teaching has never been easy. In the context of knowledge era schooling it is more difficult because it requires greater professionalism as teachers assume responsibility as mentors to individual students. It includes teaching the ability to recognise and understand one's moods, emotions and drives as well as their effects on others. Teachers need to be able to help young people develop self-confidence, to think before acting, to be comfortable with ambiguity and to be open to change. The key that holds this together is having the capacity to realistically engage in self-assessment.

Teachers need to possess all these attributes if they are to teach them. They also need the skill, as well as the purpose, to integrate them into their curriculum. No longer can self-awareness and self-assessment be 'hidden' in the curriculum where some might develop the intention and skill but most don't. In earlier chapters, I argued that emotional maturity and intelligence are equal to academic intelligence. In fact, they are central to the development of the key knowledge era skills of self-direction and self-management.

In many senses, we can look at the development of self-awareness and self-assessment as being akin to the traditional sense of teaching values or morality. It is more realistic because it focuses on the individual developing what is right for them and being able to apply it to relationships with others. It is within these relationships that self-awareness and assessment lead to ethical ways of working with other people.

Resiliency is an important component of individual development. It is the ability to recover strength, humour and spirit in the face of adversity. It has also been defined as the ability to bounce back after setbacks or being stressed. Young people who have life experiences that foster resiliency often differ from those who do not. They have an active approach to solving life's problems, a tendency to perceive life experiences constructively, an ability to gain the positive attention of others, and an ability to maintain a positive vision of life. New City School in St Louis (see Chapter 3) has a strong focus on Emotional Intelligence through the concept of Personal Intelligences.

We have a responsibility to provide our young people with experiences that are positive and meaningful and that will contribute to the development of resilience. It is resiliency that sets them up to cope with life in all of its joy and sadness and everything between. It is this quality of resilience that is more likely to be associated with successful outcomes in life such as higher achievement, greater satisfaction and the ability to make wise choices. This ability to make wise choices includes those made in the face of (inevitable) temptation, such as experimenting with drugs, indulging in unsafe sexual practices, gambling foolishly and indulging in the many other forms of high-risk behaviour to which children, youth and adults are exposed (Christie, 2002). Loreto Normanhurst has explored ways of helping young people develop skills for making effective choices.

Loreto Normanhurst, NSW

Loreto Normanhurst has developed a student growth model to allow students to set goals and to provide support from teachers and parents to enable them to achieve them. Underpinning the model is the FACE curriculum, which comprises faith, academic, community and extracurricular dimensions. Each student develops a growth plan and has regular meetings with an adviser. The student, their adviser and parents converse several times a year to support the process. Central to the model is the development of life-long learning skills.

<http://www.loretonh.nsw.edu.au>

While this is a good illustration of schools accepting new responsibilities in a complex world, knowledge era schooling would argue that this needs to be part of the total experiential learning throughout schooling where EQ and such skills as resiliency are fully developed.

Self-management and self-directed learning

We have talked about the role that schools should have in developing young people so that they can take ownership of their lives, accept individual responsibility, be accountable and so on. There is very little evidence that schools can effectively do this. As Drucker (2000) says, while people will have to manage themselves they are 'totally unprepared for it'. The next chapter will focus entirely on this concept.

A key component of being a self-managed person is being a self-directed learner. Managing effectively is about being able to learn and to be continuously involved in learning. Important teaching skills include not only being able to help students develop positive dispositions towards self-directed learning and the accompanying skills, but also being able to diagnose young people's stages of self-direction and plan learning experiences accordingly. As parents we also need to ask teachers how they will do this with our children.

In Chapter 8 I talked about the need to encourage a greater professional focus from teachers and I pointed to the actions that Eltham College and its teachers have taken. Teachers need to be self-managing, to have ownership of their professional roles as teachers and to be self-directed learners. This cannot happen without the support of school leadership in creating the appropriate conditions and culture. Further, we cannot expect these attributes from our young people if we as teachers and adults are not modelling it.

There are developmental stages for young people as they progress through school and we recognise that becoming self-managing is a developmental process, but individual learning programs, for example, will allow this development to be planned and to occur. There is a problem with traditional schooling as Knowles (1980) suggests. She believes that while adults are capable of self-directed learning, they have been constrained by their prior experiences as passive recipients of teacher knowledge in classrooms (Hatcher, 1997) in schools. Grow (1991) recommends that teachers learn to match learners' stages of self-direction with their learning experiences and prepare them to proceed to higher stages through the process of empowering them to become more self-directed. This means that an important teaching skill is being able to determine a young person's stage of self-direction.

In its *Blueprint for Government Schools*, the Victorian government provides a framework for an effective Victorian government school system, including key principles of teaching and learning. The principles reflect a close correlation with the key teaching skills and outcomes of knowledge era schooling, focusing on:

- teachers developing positive relationships with students
- promoting a culture of value and respect

- using strategies to promote student self-confidence and willingness to take risks with their learning
- creating a learning environment that promotes independence and motivates students to work autonomously, make decisions about what and how they learn and take responsibility for their learning.
- teaching team-building skills so students can collaborate, negotiate, contribute to joint assignments and experience the sharing of roles, responsibilities and ownership
- supporting different ways of thinking and learning
- building on students' prior experiences, knowledge and skills
- capitalising on students' experiences of a technology-rich world
- challenging and supporting students to question and reflect
- developing investigation and problem-solving skills
- fostering imagination and creativity
- connecting learning and practice with communities beyond the classroom.

<http://www.sofweb.vic.edu.au/blueprint>

We are now widely recognising that young people and their world of global knowledge have changed forever. The emerging focus to identify what teaching and learning should be is very important. The Victorian government example illustrates the importance of having government leaders setting strategic directions. In the final chapter I will suggest that effective leadership also is about making things happen, not simply developing policy.

The skills just described are not new. They integrate many of the skills that teachers have used for many years. What is at the centre in terms of using these skills, however, is attitude. Teachers need to believe that young people will respond positively and work with them. They need to want to work collaboratively with young people and be prepared to share authority. Let me give another illustration of these knowledge era teaching skills in action.

iNet Workshop, Victoria

A group of six middle years students approached a school leader saying they had enjoyed their school year, yet had certain issues about their experience that they wanted to discuss. Shortly after, a Year 11 student was talking to this school leader about wanting to do a project for her Year 12 studies involving teaching drama skills to younger groups in the school.

The two groups were asked to combine their efforts—the middle years students had feedback for their teachers, and the Year 11 student had the ability to deliver the message. The two groups then brought in two senior teacher mentors (middle years cluster leaders) to assist in preparations.

The students decided to use drama to highlight issues that existed in Years 7 and 8. Issues included greater depth of challenge, more negotiation and choice, and behaviour management.

Through the efforts of these students, a half-day workshop resulted, involving Year 7 and 8 teachers, and all the students in Year 8. In all, more than 170 people participated.

The drama, music, and school captains (Year 12) moderated the discussion, with the Year 8 group and the teacher–mentors involved in role-plays. Through these role-plays the Year 8 students introduced, demonstrated, and discussed the issues.

Case presented by students at iNET Workshop, Melbourne 2005

This is a great illustration of knowledge era schooling. Not only is it an innovative way to process student–teacher issues in an empowering and non-threatening fashion—but also the very act of conceiving, organising, and managing such an event creates an exciting and intensive learning environment for both young people and adults.

Not all teachers enjoyed it, as it was threatening—particularly the role-plays —and some of the students did not see that it would produce the outcomes they sought. However, the culture existed to allow them to take a risk and the teacher skills of collaboration, negotiation and shared leadership were needed to enable it to happen. The power of students and staff who have ownership and who are working together towards self-directed learning is very considerable and has a marked influence on the attitudes of others.

Summary

Knowledge school era criterion 5: Self-management and self-directed learning

Criterion 5 synopsis: Teaching, and classrooms, extended in concept beyond a four-walled small room, should be exciting and fun. Teachers should be challenged by the new world while challenging young people to develop problem-solving skills and ethical attitudes to use their information and skills wisely. Teachers should want to explore the opportunities and challenges of their world.

In the knowledge era teachers will be demonstrating the new skills of:

- collaboration and teaming
- sharing leadership
- negotiating to arrive at shared expectations
- engagement management (managing learning rather than classrooms)
- creating and managing knowledge
- teaching for self-awareness and self-evaluation
- teaching for self-management and self-directed learning.

11 | Self-directed learning: The key to success

With the revolution in the global labour market,
people will need to change skill sets very quickly
through immediate access to new learning.

Self-direction in practice

In the previous chapter I explored some of the new skills that teachers require. Under the title of self-management, I talked briefly about self-directed learning, that is, having the disposition and skill to be a learner for life.

A crucial issue for schooling and for society is self-management. In the knowledge era, possessing the skill to be able to manage one's living, working and playing is crucial to success as an independent contractor. At the core of self-management are the disposition and skills associated with self-direction in learning. Early learning theorists would argue that throughout schooling the adult needs to be able to 'relinquish control and assistance as soon as the child can work independently' (Berk and Winsler, 1995: 30).

All that we know about the labour market of the global knowledge economy directs attention to the multiple career changes or life–work changes that people will experience in an extended working lifetime and the need for people not only to continue to learn but also to be effective just-in-time learners. This means that with the revolution in the global labour market, people will need to change skill sets very quickly by immediate access to new learning.

People will need to be life-long learners who are willing and eager to progressively upgrade their knowledge and skills as new life–work situations demand. Changes to life–work situations are increasing rapidly and will continue to do so. Our current and traditional standard of schooling is not preparing young people with the learning disposition and learning skills to deal with it, let alone making them accustomed to living with the learning that change requires.

Self-directed learning refers to the dispositions and capabilities of learners to accept responsibility for planning, seeking out learning resources and implementing and evaluating their own learning as needed (Brookfield, 1985: 16). It is a significant factor in the concept of life-long learning (Herbeson, 1991). Self-direction within the learner is an important prerequisite for that person's ability to manage their ongoing schooling and post-school education and training. Individuals are increasingly required to exercise choice in what, when, where and how they learn. The adoption of much of the 'good-sense' in early learning theory to a whole-of-schooling understanding would see us move more rapidly to effective schooling for 21st-century young people.

However, schooling generally has failed to equip school leavers with a capability for self-directed learning. This is one of the factors in the high incidence of attrition from post-school education, particularly university courses, as learners are set free from a very controlled environment to one that demands self-direction for success. The latter is not judged in terms of the degree obtained, but how people can actually use it.

Having limited self-direction skills seriously interferes with the individual's ability to make informed and independent learning choices, since without skills in self-directed learning, individuals will generally have difficulty in recognising their own learning needs. Further, such people tend to prefer the traditional, structured learning of teachers in front of classrooms where decisions about what, when, where and how to learn are made by the teacher not the learner (Guglielmino and Guglielmino, 1991). However, the just-in-time learning that is increasingly required today cannot depend on classrooms. It must depend on self-learning and accessing what is available and, if the information is not readily available, developing your own learning opportunities by finding the appropriate resources and experiences. Many of you as adults (parents and teachers) are already in this world of just-in-time learning and you know just how difficult it is without self-directed learning skills and disposition to quickly access the right learning/training as it is required!

Grow (1991) asserted that one can be taught the skills and dispositions of self-directed learning. However, in his observation schooling does not appear to encourage self-direction. In fact, quite the opposite!

Eltham College has focused considerable attention on developing the environment, teacher attitudes and teaching skills to facilitate young people learning to be self-directed learners and to foster a genuine engagement with learning.

Eltham College City Campus, Victoria

In 1996, Eltham College launched its City Campus. Year 9 students, ready for independence, new stimulus and challenge, spent one-third of their year in the heart of Melbourne's Central Business District. Combining collaborative teamwork (for example, group projects) with independent research, the students responded, through a theme approach to their curriculum, to the city's colourful past, present and future. The themes investigated Melbourne as a visionary and liveable city.

The City Campus program quickly became a highlight of the middle school for the students who eagerly anticipated their time at the city. Once there, they were purposefully engaged in producing work of very high standard. They worked collaboratively in small teams, negotiating their learning tasks. They regularly chose to work through lunch breaks, and those who entered the program with a reputation 'for being difficult' seemed to thrive. Behaviour management issues were almost non-existent. Parents commented on their child's new-found independence and, for the first time in years, were hearing about what had happened at school that day. Teachers in the program quickly learned to move beyond the traditional transmission of information. Usually, they were scaffolding (that is, building up as in a scaffold) the students' learning experiences, they were responding to the changing world of the city on a daily basis, they were facilitating effective group work and they were learning to answer questions with more questions. Teachers were learning a great deal about motivation, engagement, integration and problem solving. They were teaming together as knowledge workers, engaged in life-long and life-wide learning and they had to change to meet student expectations.

It all sounds great, and it was.

The challenge was the transition 'back' to the traditional Year 9 program and the main campus. This was not easy, nor was it particularly successful in spite of the many strategies we tried. Students were returning to a more traditional classroom setting, where their city experience was not affirmed properly by all of their teachers. While they were welcomed back, and the experience was referred to, they also heard comments such as 'now that you're back we have to work really hard to fit in our program in only two-thirds of a year'. Skills learned at the city were not being used; there was little room for negotiation or choice, and limited opportunity for self-management. The powerful learning at the City Campus was sitting in isolation for the rest of their learning and this was a real dilemma.

It wasn't until 2001 that staff realised that they had been incorrectly framing the question about transition. They had been searching for the answers to successful transition to Year 9 at the main campus, but what they needed to do was ask why that transition needed to happen at all.

Quickly the question became 'how do we create a whole-year program where students are as engaged and challenged for an entire year as they are while at the City Campus?' The answer was obvious. Eltham College is fortunate to have 20 hectares of environmental reserve as part of its grounds. It is situated in an area rich in indigenous history, and adjacent to an area famed for its natural beauty, wineries and gourmet restaurants. Staff decided to develop a complementary program to our City Campus, located close to our main campus. A curriculum would be developed which focused on all of the elements that had delivered success in the existing Year 9 program, but this would use quite different contexts and environments to engage and challenge the students. Staff were on to a winner!

By 2003, Eltham's Year 9 program combined the existing City Campus experience with a new, innovative Environmental Program at our main campus. Students spend alternate terms at each campus working with a dedicated team of multi-skilled teachers, who also act as mentors. The program provides students with relevant, stimulating hands-on learning opportunities as they make the challenging transition to young adulthood.

The academically rigorous program promotes responsibility, self-direction and decision-making. Traditional subjects are studied within contemporary themes, such as Belonging, Tracks Winding Back, Sustainability and Community Responsibility. Visits from industry experts, commercial consultants and Indigenous advisers enhance the learning experience. Each student maintains a journal and personal web page to document this special year, and uses state-of-the-art technology, photographic and media equipment to support and present their work.

At the City Campus, students learn independence and responsibility. They become train-commuters, and learn to be safe in downtown Melbourne. They undertake in-depth assignments, visit law courts and cultural centres, confront urban environmental issues, meet business people and become involved in community issues.

The bush campus develops awareness of environmental, Indigenous and cultural issues. Learning takes place in the Year 9 Centre and throughout the environmental reserve, and includes excursions and visits by guest speakers and artists. Academic and vocational are converged to help emphasise the applied nature of learning. Students integrate core learning skills, including English and Maths, into Permaculture and they are rostered to run their own commercial coffee shop five mornings a week in the Swiper's Gully Restaurant.

From 2006, the program will be city-based with students having two brief three-week blocks in the 'bush' campus. While adding to the rich city-based experiential program, this will also provide a more critical mass of teachers to better exploit the interdisciplinary nature of Victoria's new Essential Learning Standards.

As Leah said in her communication to teachers in the senior school at the conclusion of her Year 9 experience:

> We like to be consulted on problems that concern us rather than decisions being made for us. We also don't want to be treated like kids anymore … We need to have a chance to continue the skills we learnt in Year 9, such as networking and finding our own resources as well as traditional learning … We need opportunities to be independent and interact with adults

Many current education practices in schools and also universities, however, do more to perpetuate dependency than to create self-direction (Grow, 1991: 127). Young people have become very dependent on their teachers and lecturers. This can be particularly true of traditional Independent and Catholic schools (particularly single-sex schools) and public selective schools where there is little teaching for independence (*The Age*, 6 April 2005).

Grow (1991) has argued that being a dependent learner can be very limiting in terms of how that person manages life and work. Becoming an adult does not automatically make one capable of self-directed learning. Skills and dispositions for self-directed learning have to be acquired to support life-long learning. However, Grow argued that there was a strong attitude in schools that students are not mature enough for self-direction and so teacher/school direction is continued in a strongly controlled fashion. Without opportunity within school, particularly freedom to learn to make decisions, maturity and self-direction cannot be fully developed.

From as early as the 1960s, strategies to increase the level of readiness for self-directed learning have been suggested by many (Tough, 1967; Knowles, 1975; Brockett and Heimstra, 1991; Candy, 1991; Grow, 1991; ANTA Report, 1997; Warner and Christie, 1998). Knowles (in Hatcher, 1997) has supported Eltham College's approach with Year 9, suggesting that those who need to become more self-directed in learning should be teamed with those who can share and help in the experience. The teacher can be instrumental in building self-help teams as a start. The Year 9 project teams are a very good example of self-help teams where young men and women work together to manage their project. Learning situations, like the City Campus, that require certain new or additional knowledge or skills become motivating factors for young people. Eltham College's experience also points to the increasing success and engagement of young men in such teaming environments.

Teachers in the Year 9 program re-conceptualised their own roles from transmitters of knowledge and assessors of learning to organisers of self-directed learning experiences, guides and illuminators. Young people became more aware of their learning strengths, weaknesses and self-imposed barriers (such as confidence) to learning. An understanding of the conscious and unconscious processes by which learning occurs is an important start—that is, we do not leave young people in the dark about how their learning occurs. We need to talk with them and help them understand how they learn. The development of a school culture that encourages independence and self-direction is essential for this. Such a school culture makes sure that young people understand how they learn and it creates the learning opportunities that young people need to become self-directed learners. This is the 'stuff' of good school reporting, not grades and percentages.

I recently read an article by Ray McNulty, formerly Commissioner of Education in Vermont and now a senior fellow at the Gates Foundation and President of the Association for Supervision and Curriculum Development. In it, he reinforces the notion of self-directed learning. He argues, 'The ability to learn far outranks the ability to store knowledge for an assessment.' However, he believes that in education we have moved into the 'assessment era', not the 'learning era'. He recognises the importance of assessment if it informs future actions, but believes that if we cannot use it, then it only has historic value. This notion of an 'assessment era' is particularly true of senior schooling in Australia and is becoming increasingly so at other stages!

We are familiar with assessment and take comfort in it and its grades, marks and comments. However, McNulty concludes, 'In the end it is all about learning, not teaching and not assessment. In this world filled with abundant information and changes at lightning speed, the ability to learn is what will matter most in the years ahead.'

Commitment to teaching for self-direction

Self-directed learning, when used in schools, is a phrase that can excite as it is at the crux of life-long learning, but, at the same time, it can create confusion, misunderstanding and even some anxiety. The anxiety comes from parents and teachers because self-direction was rarely part of their experience when at school and it has not been a major focus of their working lives.

Schools need to commit to teaching for self-direction and creating the learning experiences and learning culture so that young people want to engage in learning. Wanting to engage is the key to becoming a self-directed learner. It creates the disposition to want to be a successful learner. This is about developing a real 'love of learning' through embracing school as a good experience. It is where the fun should come into schooling.

Eltham College: The History Centre

Students in Years 3 and 4 gain a fascinating insight into the early days of European Settlement in the History Centre. Students and teachers create spectacular historic environments of the *Endeavour*, early Sydney town and the goldfields. An innovative, dramatic simulation allows teachers and students to role-play, negotiating their way through realistic historical events of early pioneer and convict life. The program promotes hands-on independent learning and integrates the wider curriculum to include journal keeping, numeracy, art, music and Mandarin Chinese.

Teachers act as facilitators, asking leading questions and guiding frameworks. In role, they are commissioners—government workers in charge of assay prices etc. They are an unhappy lot, often gruff and authoritative. They are bad-tempered and shout a bit! One student in role noticed how unhappy one of the commissioners seemed to be so she started writing love letters to the commissioner. Not one of the teachers had anticipated this! The commissioner responded and within two weeks had received a proposal of marriage. A group of ten or so students planned all aspects of the wedding including costumes, period music, invitations and the actual ceremony. Every member of the community had an assigned role on the day.

Curriculum outcomes evolved rapidly to match the changing daily events, so writing styles incorporated letters of invitation, etc. Everyone involved will remember the wedding, its lead-up period, the context and the characters. Teachers and students together seized the magic moments and created a learning-rich spectacle.

Warner and Maher, 2005

Anxieties can enter the fray when people misunderstand what self-directed learning means. These can be increased further when the big picture, for example, gets lost in the demands of doing final year examinations and gaining tertiary entrance scores. I have had parents ask whether it means that kids in Prep have to learn for themselves and whether they are too young. Eltham's Early Learning Centre Coordinator describes it very well in relation to early learning:

> Children are encouraged to make a choice by selecting the area in which they will work. While working in these areas teachers encourage children to develop independent self-directed learning skills by actively and consciously providing opportunities for children to make decisions, think about the materials they need, ask questions and solve problems. Through this process children begin to gain an understanding of their own abilities and learn more about themselves and how they learn.

This is supported by the following early learning illustration:

The Restaurant

The early years philosophy at Eltham College celebrates the importance of play, encouraging children to discover, question and create, and to investigate possibilities about themselves and their world. In 2004, staff in the Early Childhood Centre and Prep 'imagined' a curriculum focus called 'From Earth to the Table' and arranged a visit to the Hospitality Centre. Outcomes they desired included multi-aging, collaboration, ownership by students and self-direction of learning, looking at food and produce as the content area.

What emerged from the visit was the students' desire to run their own restaurant. This was not what the teachers had imagined at all. Further discussion with the students revealed a determination to make the project succeed; the staff jumped on board and great things started to happen. Students even as young as these had quite a good sense of what might be involved in running a restaurant, and working committees quickly were formed covering vital areas such as invitations, waiters, cooks, publicity, etc. Possibilities for parent involvement were explored informally at first, with staff and parents attending a dinner in the Hospitality Centre, and this quickly blossomed into full-on support and involvement by parents who worked with the students and teachers on committees, working bees, etc.

A key principle at work was the teacher letting go and allowing the students to set the directions. Teachers as facilitators believe in the capacity of their students. They do not supply answers, nor do they believe that there is a correct answer. They talk constantly with each other, embedding fully into their work an 'action—reflection' cycle that operates seamlessly within the program but is a constant focus for formal staff meetings. As facilitators, teachers foster collaborative learning skills such as listening, modelling, negotiation and recognising strengths. Questions like 'Who can write?', 'Who can do borders?' and 'What words should we use?' were commonplace within the activity groups.

The project culminated in a wonderful 'restaurant morning' where the students invited their families to a totally student-run eating experience. Not one person doubted the rich learning that had occurred for each learner, both young and old.

It is worth noting the enormous value of this story in illustrating much of what is considered to be of significant value in the learning equation for the 21st century. Students are engaged, they make choices and negotiate, they have time to tackle a big project and see it through to completion, they use authentic assessment, and they apply their existing knowledge and extend it. The project is dynamic, demanding interconnectedness. It allows for both individual and team learning where the expressive and imaginative domains are engaged. Students learn to view and interpret reality from different stances. Teachers facilitate learning, fostering engagement and connection. They cater to individual strengths, recognising multiple intelligences and different learning styles. They share in the learning, inviting further exploration by the students. They seize the 'magic moments' recognising the breakthroughs in the group. They exercise control over themselves and their work, not over the students.

Warner and Maher, 2005

I have had a Year 11 student confront me with: 'I want to be told exactly what to learn, when to learn it and how to learn it. I want to be told what to do, when and how. Don't give me self-direction. I am still a kid.' I have had a parent say about her Year 12 son, 'But he is still a child. He needs to be told what to do.' Another said, 'I want to know when she doesn't hand in her work, but I also want you to give her another chance.' Another parent asked, 'But isn't self-direction just an excuse to not do any work or not go to class?'

I was at dinner earlier in the year and one of the guests was a parent whose son had finished Year 12 last year at a highly respected independent school. The parent told me that they had been phoned each time an assignment was due, if an assignment was late, when an assessment was to take place and so on. The parent also said, 'But I don't know how my son will go at university because all his life he has been told what, how and when to learn.'

Some people have more trouble than others in accepting the notion of self-direction as 'real' learning. Clearly, we are a society in transition to accepting the knowledge era implications for schooling.

Gaining acceptance

Marketing the notion of the development of young people as self-directed learners through a genuine, collaborative partnership within schools between teachers, students and parents as a key to the knowledge paradigm is new and difficult. It is in stark contrast to the media-dominated focus on traditional outcomes for schools—tertiary entrance scores. Important though these are, given the shortage of university places and the high level of competition, they deny the realities of the changes occurring in society, particularly the labour market. They do not recognise the demands that the new knowledge world will make of young people, who must emerge from secondary school thinking like self-managing independent contractors, who must be able to self-learn and self-direct, and who must be comfortable with and responsive to change.

Students, as they progress through school, need to reject their personal 'help-lessness', start to own their lives and decisions, and accept responsibility for them-selves and their level of success. Schooling in the knowledge era means helping them to understand the importance of information, how to access information and having enough information so that they can make decisions for themselves and create their own success. We should not be hearing, 'But some students cannot learn this way.' We are talking about the essential life–work skills for the knowledge worker.

Each student must learn to learn as a self-directed learner and each teacher must be able to teach those skills. For the majority of students this is straightforward because it simply reinforces the learning skills they have developed as 'Internet kids'. Those who seek to be directed tend to be those who have a limited, short-term view of their aspirations and want teachers to direct them towards what they need to know to attain maximum results from final examinations. These students are often the ones who have the most difficulty successfully adjusting to post-school study and work. They are more likely to change courses or even drop out because they selected their university courses based on their tertiary entrance score not on their personal interests and real capabilities (Monash University study reported in *The Age*, 6 April 2005).

Let me illustrate further:

Self-paced learning in senior years

Senior students who study Multimedia work towards a dual credential by success-fully completing their studies. In addition to contributing to the Equivalent National Tertiary Entrance Rank (ENTER), used by tertiary institutions as part of their selection, the successful student develops work-related competencies and skills and receives a nationally recognised Certificate III in Multimedia.

Students provide evidence of their competency in a variety of nominated skills by completing a series of assessment tasks. For his Write, Content and Copy unit of competency requiring him to write for Multimedia within a design focus, David worked with a 'client', a staff member with responsibility for the Care Program in the senior years, to develop a Care web site.

The process involved an initial interview with the client, a response by David to the brief that was confirmed by the client, then a series of mock-ups in his visual diary as he worked towards the finished product that can be seen at <http://www.elthammultimedia.com\davidy>. This competency has a notional time allocation of 50 hours. Although David's timetable shows Multimedia as one of his subjects, he is not required to be 'in class' at that time. He may be meeting with his client, he may be working elsewhere in the school, and he might even be doing French. He works in a self-paced environment where he manages his time and the available resources to get the work done.

His Multimedia classroom operates as a drop-in studio, where he has access not only to the hardware and software needed to complete the task, but also to qualified staff with whom he can consult. They may offer extended hours as the deadline for competencies approaches. David owns his work; he accepts accountability for managing himself. He knows, however, that he can access any amount of support from his teachers and other critical adults in his world. He knows that there is a 'safety net' should he make mistakes or poor decisions.

His issues will not be solved for him, but his teachers and mentors will work with him to identify the problems, scope a range of strategies to address these problems and set up an action plan to implement the best strategy. Life after school will expect him to have these skills, whether he enters the workforce or further study.

Warner and Maher, 2005

Most young people come to school and then enter high school, well on their way to being successful self-directed learners. They want to be engaged and they want to use the skills, technology and multimedia that have become part of this world. This is where teachers come in as working partners and together they can fine-tune the skills of self-direction and enhance the disposition to learn.

Parents supporting self-direction

Parents need to ask whether they want their sons or daughters to finish school wanting to be learners, to successfully manage their own learning throughout life and to have strong life–work skill and knowledge.

Invariably, the answer will be 'Yes', and the school's job is to provide the environment of exploring, risk-taking, innovation and change in which it can be learned. As a parent, you really don't simply want them to get to the next stage without their having the attitude and skills to be successful there!

We sometimes rationalise by saying that students learn differently and that self-directed learning doesn't suit all young people. In fact, self-direction generally has not been attractive to most Australian learners (ANTA, 1997; Warner, Christie and Choy, 1998). It is easier to be directed. This is why we have to reinforce self-directed learning skills and young people's genuine engagement all the way through a student's learning experiences at school from the early years on. In fact, the earlier we can start teaching self-direction by continuing to provide the experiences, the more tangible are the outcomes and the less anxious are students and parents. Again, this directs attention to the early learning theory of scaffolding and Vygotsky's (Berk and Winsler, 1995) Zone of Proximal Development that defines the learning relationship as the young person increasingly assuming ownership of learning.

Self-direction in formal learning can be a challenging concept for families. If young people have not had self-direction reinforced through the early and junior years and only experience it for the first time when they start secondary school, it can be difficult to watch them struggle at times and sometimes even harder to step back as parents to let them figure it out themselves.

We recognise that parents need skills and support to promote self-direction in their children. This is part of the extended role of the school. The school has a responsibility to inform and teach parents and provide opportunities for them to question, debate and learn. Eltham College has introduced parent forums within each of the school sections. These provide opportunities for parents to question and seek answers. This is where the school has to be transparent in talking about what it does and why it does it. It can be threatening, particularly at first and with some very vocal, traditional parents. The transparency is important. As well as the direct personal contact through forums, interviews and an open door policy, Eltham College's Intranet, the Knowledge Network, allows parents to find all curriculum information and access continuous reporting and communication. Parents are not only involved but also they have to participate, even if it is through the Internet at work.

Eltham College's experience with younger parents, in particular, indicates that they recognise the changed nature of the national and international labour market, the effects of globalisation, and the influence of technology in shaping socioeconomic conditions. Given that many of them have first-hand knowledge of these changes, they recognise that schooling for their children must be different from their own schooling. While they generally are not initiators of the changes in schooling, they have quickly come to recognise that schooling must reflect the real world and provide greater relevance and more particularly, life–work skills. They have then become strong supporters of schooling change.

Teachers have to accept that they are teaching for the new world of young people and the youth labour market. They have to become learners again and recognise that their job description has changed. I have a strong belief in teachers' capacity to change and to think through the implications of the new world. Eltham College has asked so much of its teachers and they have gone beyond what could be regarded as normal.

I suspect that it is less an issue for teachers and more an issue for principals, school councils, school systems and government ministers and their advisers. The last four groups still control teachers and generally they want a safe environment where the 'boat is not rocked too much'. So, my advice to parents is to challenge these groups first before challenging teachers who can only be as good as their school or system allows them to be. We need to ask whether schools provide the same opportunity for innovation, risk-taking and job ownership for teachers as they expect teachers to provide, at least in theory, for students.

Teaching for self-direction

We need to recognise that teaching for self-direction is not easy. Like all learning, it is not told one day and learned and practised the next. Changes in disposition and behaviour take time to develop once they have been lost. My earlier illustration suggests that young people start school with a disposition towards and the skill for learning to be self-directed, but as time passes schooling tends to replace this with teacher-direction and, therefore, we have to start all over again. This means unlearning as well as learning. The positive is that this involves change and so young people continue to experience how to work with change. A total school culture of self-direction makes it easier as the culture expects to continually deal with changes in attitude and behaviour as young people come to terms with the new demands on how they learn as they progress through school.

One of the most difficult issues associated with learning to be self-directed is that it cannot easily be taught in a nice, easy transition from more directed to more self-directed. Teachers and schools have always believed the opposite—that is, give students small doses of freedom and self-direction until they are ready. In simple terms, this is part of the overall problem with schooling.

Schools generally believe that learning can be controlled and managed through age groups defined in year levels. Maturation variation is enormous and so each year level ends up being managed against the constraints imposed by the least developmentally mature. The rest suffer the controls that have been created for the minority.

Schools need to provide the freedom to learn for the majority and develop the strategies for assisting the minority to grow with their new freedoms. The experience of most schools providing special programs for Year 9 would suggest that this works, as at Bellarine Secondary College in Victoria.

Bellarine Secondary College, Victoria

'We are interested in helping these students to manage themselves,'—Tim Gilley, Project Manager, Victorian Schools Innovation Commission.

Bellarine Secondary College has its own vineyard and is soon to open its own winery. There is a strong hands-on, engaged focus for Year 9 where the school recognises that Year 9 is about engaging young people in learning and feeling good about themselves as learners. In addition, networking with the local industry is helping open up career pathways for young people.

Bellarine runs agricultural and horticultural classes for students from Years 9–12. As a major innovation, students are able to determine their own project and negotiate its feasibility. This also gives them greater control over their time in learning. Associate Professor James Ladwig, University of Newcastle who is advising Victoria's Year 9 Steering Committee suggests that Year 9 is a bit of a 'no man's land' for many students. He says: I think it was best expressed by one student who said 'In Year 7 we learned how to do secondary school; in Year 8 we get good at it, and in Year 9, we do it all again.' I think it is crucial at this time in their development to get these kids involved in projects that are meaningful to them.

The Sunday Age, 27 March 2005

An important element for knowledge era schooling is relevance. Learning has to be meaningful to young people and their world. Converging academic and vocational studies, often through applied learning, also adds significantly to student engagement and success. Together these initiatives help develop young people who are more self-managing.

One of the key fears that schools, indeed parents, have is that of discipline. Take away the traditional controls and there will be students who push the boundaries. They have never been taught to deal with school freedom or good relationships, so when they have the opportunity for these some will overreact. This is a natural response, but it is very hard to help teachers and parents accept that the majority will work their way through it and succeed. The keys are patience, developing relationships and introducing adult community consequences.

Eltham College has focused on two things: the process of teaching for self-direction, which I have described in this chapter, and milestones—tangible pieces of evidence that self-direction is being developed. For example, in Year 9, students select, after a detailed process of information giving and life–work counsel (with their parents too), a set of studies for Year 10 that reflects their and our understanding of their abilities and aspirations. More sophisticated examples could include: a Year 11 student doing two Year 12 subjects and deciding to focus 90 per cent of effort in terms 3 and 4 on these to get a high examination result and simply doing enough to satisfy the requirements for the Year 11 subjects; a Year 10 student determining a vocational future and completing both the final schooling credential (in Victoria the Victorian Certificate of Education) and a Vocational Certificate III by the end of Year 11; a Year 5 student having a set of work commitments on a Monday and completing them with minimal parent/teacher encouragement by Friday; a Year 8 team of students deciding to produce and direct a play with minimal teacher assistance, to illustrate their understanding and enjoyment of the piece of literature they have been studying.

An example of a failed milestone could be a Year 11 or 12 student who decides to miss a piece of assessment because they have not done the work and complaining when they fail that learning outcome or getting a parent or even a doctor to offer up excuses for them.

Melinda Scash, team leader of a Year 7–8 cluster and now teaching in Queensland, prepared the following parent guidelines to explain how self-directed learning operates in the middle years:

In middle schooling self-directed learning relies on:

- close working with individuals
- skill development
- open relationships
- open communication
- carefully structured learning experiences which maximise student access to success
- negotiation
- teachers responding to the needs and interests of students
- training for decision-making

- engagement and purpose
- support from teachers and parents
- developing time management skills
- a teacher belief in student ingenuity, passion and capability
- flexibility
- goal setting and learning how to set goals and then achieving them
- relevance of the curriculum and learning experiences
- a shared valuing of life-long learning.

For example, as students are encouraged to make choices about how to use the available class time teachers will monitor the effectiveness of the student's approach. In Year 7 a major task may be required in stages, or the process may include scheduled conferencing between teacher and student. This ensures that those students, who are not used to managing their own learning, don't fall behind. Students who need help may be provided with a series of explicit procedural steps. Students who are able to demonstrate more self-direction in learning can take more responsibility for designing and programming their learning activities. This training for self-directed learning requires a lot more of the teacher and the student but has immeasurable benefits when students embrace proactive learning for life.

This form of teaching, including continuous reporting through the intranet, demands much more of a teacher than does traditional teaching. Directed teaching, associated with strong classroom management and a school-supported 'punishment' system, is much easier than a school that encourages innovation and demands that students learn to be self-directed learners, innovators, entrepreneurs and partners in learning. It is so much easier to treat a young person as a child than as a person. It won't be for much longer. Increasingly we see young people reacting and sometimes retaliating because their world and the traditional world of schooling are in contrast and conflict (Slade, 2001).

Year 10 students are not children nor are they quite adults, although they are closer to the latter than the former. This is a year in which greater exploration in learning will occur. Eltham College has put Year 10 into the Senior School, reflecting their status in society and recognising that they are no longer middle school 'kids'. Reasonably, staff knew that they could not provide the year-long experience for Year 9 independent of the rest of the school and then put Year 10 back into middle school. After all, most are beyond the age of compulsory schooling. They have seven units or subjects per semester and some have their seventh as Hospitality at night or Horticulture in the afternoon. The reduction in class time gives Year 10 'spare' time, that is, free periods. This is very deliberate and part of their transition into accepting greater responsibility for themselves. There are teachers available to provide support, but students learn to make their own decisions about using their time and most will be found at different times chatting with friends, doing assignments or homework, visiting the café, perhaps playing some sport or spending time talking with their mentors.

Schools associated with the Specialist Trust Schools in the United Kingdom offer many illustrations of transformation and innovation. Dartford Grammar is focusing on both space and varied learning activities to promote self-direction:

Dartford Grammar, UK

Developing approaches to teaching and learning for learning autonomy

The school is renovating space to provide accommodation for its Sixth Form, based around an Internet-café and providing more flexible learning/studying areas designed to suit students' learning styles and to allow a more autonomous approach to learning.

The project is a long-term (and ongoing) development aimed at reviewing teaching and learning in KS5 and the environment in which this happens.

An initial review of our Sixth Form provision (in January 2003) suggested that much of our teaching and students' learning is too teacher dependent and limited by the physical restrictions of the school's buildings, forcing 'traditional' classes of a set size, often with many teachers within the same faculty teaching the same topics in the same ways in neighbouring classrooms.

In the light of this, some of the developments to studying in KS5 include suspending the normal timetable for IB students to allow them a week to complete their Extended Essays, including teaching the research skills required in a way more akin to university study. Students have also been encouraged to make increased use of ICT facilities – resources for students are typically emailed directly and copies of study-guides and resources are published on the school's network. Students complete their UCAS applications online and are encouraged to email work/notes to staff.

Intended Outcomes of the KS5 review and development include: to teach students in a way suited to the individual subject/topic and to students' own learning styles, rather than traditional teacher-led instruction in set class sizes; to increase student responsibility for their own work and develop them as autonomous learners; to prepare them more effectively for university/further education and the workplace.

Young people cannot learn to accept responsibility, make decisions and use time without the freedom in which these things can happen.

Schools often talk about teaching for adult decision-making, but responsible decision-making is not learned through a textbook or a lecture. People have to experience the opportunities to make decisions and to develop as self-directed learners. That also is part of why you, as parents, loosen the reins and allow your sons and daughters to go out at night and weekends on their own or with friends. Schools do the same in relation to learning, but with a strong safety net of care–mentoring underneath. Young people will make mistakes. In fact this is the only way in which we really learn, but it is important to have a trusting teacher-mentor to work through the mistakes and learn from them. A teacher-mentor's role is to help young people learn from mistakes, not prevent them from happening.

To move towards being an adult, self-directed learner is a very important part of learning. Eltham College's graduates will say that university or TAFE is not too difficult because school gave them the experiences to learn.

When parents don't help

Schools confront situations where parents don't help in two areas: firstly, in working to have students start to own and accept responsibility for themselves and their learning, of course within a context of teachers motivating, guiding and supporting; secondly, in helping students realise the full potential of their individual talents. This happens occasionally and often unwittingly. A teacher recently sent me an article along with a series of papers on gifted education. The article, 'Does criticising your child's teacher disempower your child?' by Miraca Gross (2003), reflects on the effect of parent negativity towards schools or teachers.

Miraca Gross argues from some research on gifted children that

> ... parents believed that their child's success was primarily the responsibility of the teacher, not the child ... Although these parents were concerned about their children's underachievement and wanted to help them improve, they failed to model an intrinsic motivation to achieve a desire to learn for the sheer satisfaction of learning. Additionally, the parents seldom modelled a healthy respect for school or the education system. Indeed, a substantial number of the parents were openly critical in front of their children, of teachers and of school's policies ... If parents model a belief that the education received at school is trivial, boring, or of little value, their children will develop the same attitudes ...

As a parent I know just how complex it is to be one, and how often we are criticised for our parenting skills, even though great parenting training programs are thin on the ground. However, I do know that what Gross writes about sometimes happens and it has a negative consequence. Self-direction, for example, is one of those issues. We as parents, in not understanding self-directed learning, having reservations about it, or not knowing how to support it, can actually reinforce dependence and create a negative perception in young people of the value of learning to be a successful life-long learner.

We can help by acknowledging and praising achievements and efforts and by helping young people understand that successful life–work is very much about being self-managing and being a self-directed learner. Young people are never too young to be brought into discussions about our world.

Very few of us are not aware of the 21st century's changed world of work and the demands to be continuously engaged in learning; very few of us are not aware of the problems associated with not owning your life, work and learning and having to be dependent on someone else or something else; very few of us are not aware of the influence of today's Internet, media and multimedia on how young people are developing both skills and world views. However, we sometimes are scared to move from the familiar in terms of schooling, despite the evidence that points to the new world of 21st-century learning achieving the same high outcomes that the familiar produced.

Parents need to learn to explore issues of concern with the school rather than negatively commenting on teachers or schools directly to their children. The criticism might be right but it can be better dealt with in direct contact with the school, rather than taking the risk that negative comments may in fact be negating important and substantial learning opportunities.

The key to our future

The benefits of self-directed learning will not only meet students' immediate needs for accomplishing their formal learning goals, but also prepare them for life-long learning. The added investment that schools and governments can make into enhancing the dispositions and skills for self-directed learning will support the need in the Australian workforce for knowledge workers, potentially reduce school and post-school dropout rates and help bring about the schooling change essential to matching schooling with the new world in which we all live.

Self-directed learning is critical not only to being an effective participant in the knowledge era, but also to surviving in an environment that continues to be profoundly influenced by economic, technological and social changes (Drucker, 1995, 2000). While Knowles (1997) predicts that by year 2020 all learning will be based on principles of self-directed learning and Beare (2003) would support this, I am arguing that to simply let it evolve over the next fifteen to twenty years is to ignore the young people of today. Parents, through their influence, cannot afford to ignore their own children and leave the essential changes, particularly self-directed learning, for the next generation. Given the nature of the global knowledge economy that may well be too late for Australian young people and for Australia.

It can be argued that Eltham College's parents and students have come to see self-directed learning as the key outcome from schooling. Independent parent and student surveys direct attention to very positive feedback: parent forums and focused independent surveys have become very supportive and positive. In the Year 7–8 Parent 2004 Survey, the researcher said:

> A number of findings of this report are providing very specific and real support for this notion that knowledge era culture is becoming part of the Eltham parent experience. More than two-thirds of parents rated the development of self-direction as one of the two most desirable goals for their child. The second most desirable goal was creative and innovative individuals.

Professor Hedley Beare describes the future:

The old steps-and-stages, linear and age-cohort-based approach to knowledge and learning has been largely abandoned in the future school. 'Class-work' and 'school assignments' less and less resemble factory jobs, that is, a regular set of work, a regular time in class or as a class, regular hours of the day committed to a subject, and a fixed place in which the work is done. The segments of the learning program are differently organised, managed, accessed and assessed, and then used. A new kind of multi-layered learning has taken over, which creatively networks a number of disciplines and areas of knowledge. It is often project-based, involves team searches and team learning, and is formulated around a search for many-levelled, analytical answers to big and interesting questions. This is currently being called the 'thinking curriculum'.

Information and data come at us from all angles in an information-rich environment. There are multiple access points, not least for each learner, and the over-riding characteristic is connectivity. So, learning means following a search trail, in the awareness that one thing will lead to another and that illuminating patterns will emerge. The student, like any other knowledge-worker, acquires the essential skills to systematise, to apply and to test, and to impose coherence on what is being discovered, synthesised, and learnt.

Inevitably, such a curriculum dwells on skills as much as on content, and emphasises the progressive deepening of the capacity for identifying and analysing a problem or issue. It leads to devising ways to solve or handle the problem, and then the application of the findings both to this problem and in other areas of knowledge and skill.

So the curriculum has become increasingly borderless and transnational. Accessing the sources both of the storage and the generation of knowledge is routine. Thus, what is to be 'learnt by heart' in the curriculum is shrinking to a core of 'knowings' tied to negotiating one's way around the global community of knowledge. That part of learning is called 'scaffolding knowledge', the frameworks that keep the structure of knowledge standing.

Beare, 2001

Most of our young people today would argue quite strongly that this is their world now and their future in this global knowledge world is dependent on our making the difference in today's world, not leaving it for fifteen years. They would hope that their parents and teachers would understand their world and help them by seeking the changes we have talked about in this chapter. Without the disposition and skill to be self-directed as learners, young people will have very limited capacity to become self-managing.

Summary

Self-directed learning, the key skill for the knowledge era is:

- having the disposition and skill to be a learner for life.
- at the core of self-management

- an important prerequisite for that person's ability to manage their ongoing post-school education and training, that is, managing their living and working
- a skill that can be developed in every individual with support from teachers and parents
- strongly linked with engagement in learning and work
- not a coming of age skill
- progressively developed with the maturation and readiness of the individual.

What to expect
from a knowledge
era school 12

Trust, honesty, shared decision-making, negotiation,
integrity and personal accountability are all essential
components that contribute to establishing an inclusive
learning environment in our schools.

Year 10—the bridge to senior school

We commence our tour in the Year 10 common area. Today, students are sitting chatting with friends, catching up on work individually or in groups, others are organising a social activity or Student Council charity event. Some are using the Internet; others are being boisterous, even unseemly to adult ears, or are outside on the basketball court expending energy shooting hoops. Some students might be in the library, the multimedia laboratory or in some other specialist area and most are in classes. So often they are using the common areas to authenticate their work with others: interviewing, making a movie, preparing presentations, but they will all take some time to 'goof off'.

They are generally 15 years of age, even 16, with about 10 per cent still to turn 15. They are young adults. They have freedoms—spare lessons—as part of their planned curriculum. This is where they learn to balance life and work, to make decisions about how they will spend their time and become accountable for their own achievements, and to manage time. They also have time to see mentors (called LifeWork Coaches) to discuss issues confronting them or go to the Senior School Café for a latte. They are friendly, unabashed and happy to talk with our visitors about their first year as senior students. They greet us, usually by first names, and the visitors and ask how we are. They are better able to describe their learning and their responsibilities as developing self-directed learners.

Visitors tend to baulk just a little when we first walk into the Year 10 common areas. They are generally noisy, somewhat untidy; the students are physically large and they are quite 'in your space' when they greet you. However, the visitors listen to what we are about and talk with these confident and open young people, leaving the area feeling that they have learned something new and valuable. Some visitors may not be entirely comfortable, but a recent survey of Eltham College's Year 11 people on their Year 10 experiences suggested:

- They recognise that their teachers generally treat them like young adults, but they were conscious that sometimes, as students, they behaved like little kids.
- The 'teacher factor' is seen as critical by all of them. Most of them referred to the notion of good relationships with their teachers and many mentioned that they liked the more informal environment, using their teachers' first names, etc.
- All spoke passionately about the role of the teacher in creating a successful learning environment. A good teacher sets high expectations. They believe that the teacher factor is always important, and that a strong passion for a subject could overcome a poor relationship.
- They acknowledge the broad range of subjects on offer. They like the balance of VCE, Vocational and Year 10 subjects. They were pleased with their subject allocations generally, and with the process of subject selection.
- They valued the opportunity to make changes to subject selections, citing reasons such as wrong or poor choice, mismatch of teacher style and their own learning preferences.
- They commented on the increased workload in Year 10 though many saw that this was inconsistent across different classes/subjects. What they saw as the biggest factor in increased workload was their realisation that they finally had to do it for themselves. One person commented that this could be overwhelming and emotionally demanding, indicating that we still have a long way to go in developing learning ownership as young people work through school.

Years 11 and 12—tomorrow's workforce

Our tour moves on to the roomy area where Years 11 and 12 share lots of common study space. A combined Study Studio for young people doing Unit 3/4 studies includes about 40 PCs for work and Internet access at small workstations. They greet visitors in an easy, laidback fashion but then quickly return to their work, generally individually, but often in small groups. It is a little noisy and fairly untidy, but they are engaged as their very high level mid-year VCE exam results confirm. About ten of them are outside sitting on easy chairs talking and sharing notes, and they always offer a good chat to visitors. They will also joke, 'Oh, we are self-directed … as you can see!' This is healthy and adds to the authenticity of the relationships between staff and students as well as to the authenticity of developing self-directed learners. Increasingly, the school is breaking down the barriers of senior year levels in creating an adult, campus environment for senior schooling.

One of our Year 12s, Leigh, featured in a newspaper column with several other students from Victoria. In his most recent column he said:

> Over the term two holidays this year I went to England and the US as part of the Youth Leaders International (YLI), an international program that involves students aged 15 to 18.
>
> I stayed in London for a week with my family before meeting up with the YLI at Cambridge University for the Life Skills Training conference of 2004, alongside students from Romania, China, Russia, Israel, Australia and the Dominican Republic.
>
> After the conference YLI invited me to be a guest speaker at a function in Washington DC, where I spoke to other students about a charity pushbike ride I did from Melbourne to Sydney in Year 10 to raise money for Kids Under Cover.
>
> On the way home from Washington, I had a 23-hour stopover in Los Angeles and was lucky enough to see 1980s metal legends WASP at the House of Blues club.
>
> Getting back to school was good as I had been away for a whole month. I had missed out on only one SAC and, surprisingly, there wasn't a great deal to catch up on. I've started summarising the year's work in all my subjects and am looking forward to the holidays in September when I can really get organised and put in a lot more study.
>
> *The Herald Sun,* 2004

There is a big world out there for young people. Not all can have Leigh's experiences in Year 12, but most will have similar experiences over time. Leigh's descriptions direct attention to knowledge era schooling. He didn't miss much because his learning is flexibly structured. Perhaps even more telling is that Leigh is in control and managing what he needs to do. His is not pressuring himself to achieve the highest possible tertiary entrance because he knows exactly what he needs and how to get it. This is maturity in learning or, in other words, a successful self-directed learner. Many young people in senior school are able to manage their timetables to fit in with their other commitments; all have a social calendar, many work, a number are elite athletes who need time and space to combine school and work (which is their sport).

In the knowledge era school young people will take a more mature and knowledgeable approach to their life–work ambitions and selection of post-school courses. They will select subjects that suit them and select post-school courses appropriate to them and that they want to do. They will not scramble for the highest tertiary entrance scores and go into whatever courses the score allows, often associated with the causes of university dropout. They will aim for what they need. This is a mature approach for 17- to 19-year-olds. This is not a cop-out for seeking something less than excellence. They are engaged and they put enormous effort into their work, particularly those subject areas most relevant to their post-school choices. They can still be here into the night enjoying their project or assignments. This is engagement. It is not about simply working to achieve the highest possible tertiary entrance score. It is working to fulfil their interests and goals. They also will talk to visitors about their part-time work and other family, sport, cultural and social commitments.

Eltham College's four captains in 2004 organised a conference of forty-five school leaders from eleven other schools and together they came up with a 'Youth Vision for Schooling Statement' that they have presented to the Victorian Minister for Education. It made a very powerful statement in terms of school relationships:

Curriculum

It is imperative that schooling changes with the times, keeping up with the pace that the modern world is setting. Gone are the days when core subjects represented the entirety of a school's curriculum. Students must be able to choose subjects that suit their needs, goals and interests. For this to happen, curricula need to grow and branch out into new directions, so that students can choose subjects that are relevant to the time and to their lives. Today, information technology is no longer a learning supplement, but a necessary and integral part of providing students with skills for the future. Providing flexibility is also essential, moving away from the rigidity that has defined school curricula in the past, encouraging diversity of education and allowing students to develop a set of skills, matched to their own interests, complementing their schooling but as a part of their life-long learning.

The 2005 Captains organised a second such conference and engaged the Federal Minister for Education, Science and Training in debate about schooling and the government's directions. Again, the findings of the conference have been shared with government and other schools.

Our senior students look in the faces of visitors and say that their external examination results are as good if not better than previous years when more traditional approaches were used. Not quite convinced, a visitor asks: 'Can young people really have all this freedom and still achieve?'

Parents do need to understand that learning in the knowledge era school *is* structured. Young people expect structured, concrete and experiential learning and to reap the consequences if they do not make the effort or achieve the outcomes. Once experiences relevant to the learning outcomes or objectives are negotiated and in place, there are two major activities: first, a structure where time-lines and expectations are put into place, and; second, consequences that are clearly defined.

With support, lots of it early in schooling and less as young people grow in their skills and engagement, students manage this learning, generally within a team, and learn to be learners. Consequences will be varied across developmental stages in the school and can include: loss of own time to catch up, interview with parents or losing a privilege, and at the senior end, a failure. However, most consequences are positive and designed that way. If the learning objectives are achieved as negotiated, there are rewards such as free time, opportunities to extend the activity in unusual ways, and always praise or, in senior schooling, just simply self-satisfaction. This also involves positive continuous reporting both to young people and their parents. We report online, so this positive information goes home quickly and regularly.

Respecting student voice

Our tour continues past the Senior School Café where young people and staff can take a break and catch up on the day's events over a latte in a similar environment to the one they will find at a tertiary institution or in the workplace. Inside, two students are seated at a table making notes in preparation for their involvement in a working party meeting at lunchtime. Here again, the knowledge era school looks for opportunities to integrate school learning experiences with the realities of our lives. Working parties consisting of both young people and staff look at issues together. Recently, student representatives from a Behaviour Management Working Party presented the party's findings to staff and outlined the resultant new expectations regarding Setting the Classroom environment as follows:

- Staff to set classroom vision collaboratively with students, bearing in mind we are a PeaceBuilders® school
- Refer to Rights and Responsibilities document (see appendix to full set of recommendations), keeping in mind that we are 'individuals achieving together'
- Students need to be aware that we are all accountable to legal constraints and Occupational Health and Safety requirements, and that there will be times when teachers need to insist on certain courses of action
- Examples—What would you like your classroom to be like? How would you like to be treated … by me, by others? What would make you look back and say 'This was a great class'?

We hear other students in the café discussing International Relations, a small group departs to work in the science lab with visiting chemistry academics and others from Student Council are organising a fashion festival for 1000 people to raise funds for a charity. A group is playing pool and another is planning a concerted campaign through the Student Council to have greater access to games on the Internet during their time allotment.

There is strong evidence that the effect of knowledge era schooling is learning and confident, successful people working together. These young people will demonstrate an understanding of change and their comfort with it. Through knowledge era schooling young people believe that they can make a difference and if something needs to change they can help make it happen.

Although we consider our environment to be relaxed, visitors typically describe it as business-like, where young people and older people are engaged in working. Why would people say it is business-like? Generally, because they see it in the same way as the real world outside of schools operates. It is not managed in classroom-type settings with a supervisor at the front (that was the industrial world of work some 30 years ago). People work in teams and individually, sometimes in both. In fact, they often work in several teams, including virtual teams through the Internet. They do a lot of collaborating, as we do in homes and communities.

The LifeWork Centre— making sense of life and work

We take our visitors past the café to the LifeWork Centre. Inside, young people work with the LifeWork Counsellors, traditionally called career counsellors, but in keeping with the changed post-school learning and labour market for young people, we have emphasised the life-long connections of living and working. This process starts at a very young age. At Year 2 (7–8 years of age), for example, students, with their teachers, regularly complete a reflection process on what they have learned. They then take this home to work through an additional reflection process. In class they explore what they have learned from this and how it relates to the bigger world. They develop their own résumés of experiences and skills.

Care and mentors—a vital safety net

As our tour progresses, we pass a Year 10 student chatting with a LifeWork Coach (mentor) in a small meeting room. All students have access to a LifeWork Coach and referral to professional counsellors where needed. The care/mentor program provides a safety net. Young people take risks, they make mistakes and they experience freedom because without it they will never grow into the creative, entrepreneurial young people who will challenge life. When they fall over, and fall over they must, the LifeWork program is there to help them own the mistake, work through the issues and find solutions through problem solving. In Senior School, the care program is one of transition from the closer care of a school to the post-school environment where you have to decide to seek care yourself and feel comfortable doing it.

Perhaps Alyssa (Year 8) sums it up: 'When you decide what and how you want to learn, you have a responsibility to engage in it.'

Young people throughout the secondary sections of the school will talk openly about the mentors or in senior school, their LifeWork Coaches. Some will talk positively in terms of the help they have received; others will say that their mentors were really never needed. However, we will all talk about the issue of emotional intelligence and the part that mentors play in formally ensuring that EQ is part of the young person's curriculum and schooling outcomes.

As Lauren (Year 8) said: 'We never take for granted the way the school respects us.' A key element of successful schooling is this element of respect. Before we ask that young people respect us we must respect them, warts and all!

Self-discipline

Our visitors observe that some of the students don't seem to be in full uniform and that jewellery is more prominent than would normally be associated with a school culture. The real issue for parents is the relationship between uniform, image and discipline. Schools are often judged on how their students wear their uniform. Poor wearing is seen as lack of pride and poor discipline. Parents get angry with schools because they cannot get their son or daughter to leave home in the appropriate uniform: 'If there were more discipline at school, I would not have this problem'. The reality is that most of us, as parents, will have issues from time to time with the clothes our sons and daughters select to wear and how they wear them, including uniform. Wearing uniform does not prepare young people for the workforce. At best, uniform can help young people in learning to be self-managed and self-disciplined. Young people need to be able to learn to make appropriate decisions about what they are wearing, not simply see what they are wearing as a matter of adult authority, rules and discipline.

In a knowledge era school, the person **in** the clothing is what is important, not what that person is wearing or how they are wearing it. There is a natural contradiction between the working together philosophy and collaboration on the one hand and, on the other hand, the enforcement of rigid uniform standards. It is difficult to say: 'Take the jewellery off, tuck in that shirt and let's collaborate in working through this project.'

Students at Eltham College appear well dressed but casual most of the time. When they are representing the school at official events on or off-campus, they are just like people in the real world of work and present themselves appropriately. Our core uniform comprises many different items, allowing students to choose from a range appropriate to their age and the activity they may engage in during the day. So, you will see some in core uniform, some with ties and some without, many in school tracksuits or sports gear and some in casual gear. Our school celebrates individuality, and we accept that young people often use clothing to define their uniqueness. Our expectations are clear, but how we handle those students who do not meet expectations is very important. We always work to communicate with the person within the uniform and to give them an opportunity to explain.

In an overt demonstration of flexibility and mutual respect, the knowledge era school lets its students work within a flexible arrangement, trusting that they will reciprocate that respect. Trust is a big word in knowledge era schooling: the knowledge era school does not create lots of rules for students or indeed for teachers, because it knows that the vast bulk of people can be trusted to do the right thing.

Relationships and engagement

At we move through the school, our visitors often comment on the atmosphere of engagement, friendliness and openness, where busy people are having fun. Often young people are on first name terms with their teachers and address older people in a very open and direct manner. If, as a visitor, you are a parent of a young person who might only be in the early years of schooling, some of this may cause shock because you are not used to dealing with young teenage people at home. However, if you are open, you will talk with them and with teachers and learn about confident young people.

The 'Youth Vision for Schooling Statement' (2004) made a very powerful statement in terms of school relationships:

RELATIONSHIPS

Relationships are a driving force and major focus area for today's young people and schools need to recognise this fact. Schools must equip students with the abilities to relate with family, friends and colleagues. The student/teacher relationship is fundamental in establishing and developing an environment conducive to learning and equipping young people with the knowledge, skills and attributes necessary to contribute fully to the society in which they live. These increasingly sophisticated relationships need to be founded on a clear set of values, which are shared and owned, by teachers and students alike. It is becoming evident in today's world that the student/teacher relationship needs to be one where respect is earned and not based on status or position. Teachers need to recognise that they too are life-long learners and should model their behaviours accordingly. Students and teachers must acknowledge the partnership they enter into and fully appreciate the need to always treat others with consideration and regard and to value and respect one another's knowledge, skills and abilities. Trust, honesty, shared decision-making, negotiation, integrity and personal accountability are all essential components that contribute to establishing an inclusive learning environment in our schools.

A technology-rich environment relevant to the knowledge era

We continue our tour and proceed to the Library–Information Services Centre. Individuals, small groups and class groups are always busy working there. There is a bustle of activity as people come and go as they do in other general areas such as computer labs, art rooms and the media centre. Young people and library staff will talk about what is happening and the services that this centre provides in supporting self-directed learning.

In one corner of the library, a teacher is working with a small group of students who are going through a self-directed online information technology subject. One young student uses the interactive whiteboard to demonstrate a new software shortcut that even his teacher wasn't aware of; his superior skill is welcomed in a supportive and non-threatening manner.

Elsewhere in the library, several young people are logged on to Knowledge Network, the college intranet. It is a technology-based enabling tool that connects students, teachers and parents in a powerful learning partnership within a secure interactive and transparent learning environment. The students may be accessing their online reports, curriculum or learning resources. Students are managing their own learning while at the same time their parents may receive an email alert that their son's or daughter's report has been updated. They can immediately access assessment results from a project online and have family discussion about it the same night.

Parent Maryanne says: 'Knowledge Network allows me to support my child's learning by giving me immediate access to the curriculum, teacher feedback and progress reports. I can really participate in her education.'

Kristy (Year 8) says: 'The Knowledge Network has so much stuff. All our coursework is there for us and you can check what's coming up. Our reports are updated all the time. We can look at them whenever we want to see how we're doing and if we need to do better.'

Young people also are engaged in 'resuméing' as part of their reports, reflecting on their progress as part of their development and communicating with teachers and parents.

Middle years—excitement is the key to engagement

From the Library–Information Services Centre we head to the middle years' area where young people are preparing to celebrate the climax of an enrichment week, an integrated learning experience that promotes in-depth work, often collaborative and usually involving four core subjects areas. Some groups have been designing roller coasters, some have been conquering a bridge building challenge, while other students have developed a play from the *Rime of the Ancient Mariner* and given public performances. A Year 8 class studying a novel, converted it into a play, and engaged their teachers and classes in art and drama and presented it over three performances to the public. Their schooling experience not only encourages initiative, creativity and risk-taking, but also creates the conditions in which these things can happen. The knowledge era school is an enabling school. Collaboration is not only a word, but also a reality of daily life.

Amy (Year 7) said, 'I never knew Maths could be interesting until I had to build a roller coaster.'

The integration of learning allows young people to understand the relationships between familiar subjects and in turn, their relationship to their world. This makes a substantial difference to how well they engage in learning.

The middle years have groups in classes and some in the common rooms working on their own material, many are in the library where working with the librarians, the IT staff and assistants is an important part of how they learn. Some students will be using the Internet or the Knowledge Network eTV, possibly watching last night's current affairs.

James (Year 7) said, 'Eltham College recognises our individual talents and supports us in pursuing our dreams.'

Our tour continues past the Year 5/6 area where learning is themed around the 'Future Zone'. The program empowers young people to have an active role in shaping their future and to take responsibility for making choices that will have a positive impact on themselves, each other and the environment. Three flexible multi-age groups work collaboratively in a two-year cycle in a stimulating space designed for open learning.

What about bullying?

As we move on, one visitor raises what is one of the most frequently asked questions on school tours: 'How does Eltham College address bullying?' Bullying is a major social issue across Western cultures. The knowledge era school does not try to gloss over such issues, but develops appropriate knowledge era responses. This includes building preventative measures and values into the culture and using accepted community practice in relation to the law and workplace health and safety regulations as logical consequences of anti-social behaviour. We used a program called Peace-Builders® to help develop a working together culture where we work on preventing anti-social behaviour rather than intervening to deal with it afterwards.

The program is based on a positive belief system that people can learn to work together and solve life's problems in a culture that promotes harmony and resilience. When we get it right in schools, we have the opportunity through our students and influence, to make a difference in the wider community and the workplace.

History comes to life in Year 3–4

We head now to the Year 3–4 History Centre where young people are engaged and having fun. Some are in one of the four classrooms attached to the open History Centre; a dramatic simulation of the goldfields is taking place with another group. Some are catching up on their journals, another group is with a teacher, and others are in the computer pod. A maintenance staff member is working with students to build the *Endeavour*'s framework. A parent is getting costumes ready for the visit to the goldfields at Sovereign Hill as Chinese coolies. We do not need to tell the visitors about their program. The kids take over to describe what it is all about, what they are learning and the whole approach of the History Centre.

Have you ever spent two years learning through the excitement and challenge of dramatic simulation? Imagine in Years 3 and 4, that you are Governor Bligh, a convict mother with a baby or Sergeant Ikin of the Rum Corps and all your engagement in learning—literacy, reading and writing your journal, numeracy, humanities, drama, science and discovery and so on—is undertaken 'in role'. The year comes to an exciting conclusion in the historic township of Sovereign Hill in Victoria with students dressed as Chinese workers who have walked from South Australia to be greeted by (role-playing) adults taunting them with racist and unwelcoming comments.

Visitors are free to stay and it is hard to move them on once they start talking with these young people and their teachers.

Year 9—open and dynamic learning

Eventually we head across the road from the main campus to the Environmental Centre, located adjacent to the 8 hectare environmental reserve, where half the Year 9 cohort are based for two terms exploring an integrated, thematic curriculum incorporating English, Maths, Science, Humanities, Language, Arts and Technology. Themes of study include making the Environmental Centre into a working model of sustainability. Some students are problem-solving—designing and installing an irrigation system; others are considering recycling issues or refurbishing an old water tank and a greenhouse.

We suggest our visitors make a time to drop into the City Campus in the heart of Melbourne's City Business District where the remaining Year 9 cohort is spending a full semester taking responsibility for themselves as daily commuters. The city is their extended classroom.

Our visitors observe the apparent lack of traditional classroom environments in the Year 9 program. Locking young people into a perpetually rigid routine tends to assume a base level of ability geared towards a certain type of student excelling in that environment. There are times when young people need and excel in the classroom setting, but just like an office, there are many activities that can and should take the student regularly out into different learning environments. Just as in the real world, life involves a variety of interactions, commitments, and deadlines that requires flexibility, responsiveness to change, and open-mindedness. Schools and their teachers need to be brave enough to allow it.

Learning for real

At the end of the tour, we encourage our visitors to call in at the Hospitality Centre/Vineyard, a few hundred metres along the road from the Environmental Centre. There the Year 9 students run a coffee shop, which is open to the public Monday to Friday from 8.30 a.m. to 11.30 a.m. The students serve customers and get immediate feedback as in real-life situations, make coffee, handle money, learn the management of a coffee shop and receive internal accreditation. Next week in the coffee shop, they will serve the Preps morning tea as the commencement of a year-long project relating to food and restaurants. The experience will lead the Preps to set up their own restaurant and prepare and serve food for their parents.

Each afternoon, senior students in Years 10 to 12 will arrive to operate the 'Swiper's Gully' training restaurant for the public five nights a week, which can have up to 65 patrons, the students preparing and serving a three-course meal, pouring wine, and delivering great service. Some are also engaged in vocational Horticulture with Viticulture, many others are doing Multimedia or Information Technology. The students are converging academic subjects with vocational.

Summary

In a world so dominated by change, the one distinguishing feature about this knowledge era school is that it will always be in transition—a transition that moves with the times. Operating from sound underlying principles, based on years of research and experience, the knowledge era school will always be ready to work with the real world of young people and the global community in which they live. Young people will always come in or move from one year to the next carrying with them their stages of development, emerging attitudes and different behaviours. They have the right to expect that we will respect that they need to work through their issues, with us working with them. The concern will never be 'getting it right' so that the next year's group of young people won't have to go through these experiences. Learning comes from the way we all work through these experiences year by year and from the early years onwards, applying the concepts of scaffolding and older person–younger person learning relationships.

The knowledge era school deals with young people as they grow to maturity in the 21st-century global knowledge society. As parents, we know that the present schooling is out of touch with both the new world and the young people who have claimed it. We know that it has to change. Eltham College and many other schools show that young people can thrive in the new knowledge era school and at the same time, achieve the outcomes, including academic, that are traditionally regarded as 'proper'. This means we are in transition and if parents and schools can collaborate, in the same way we ask teachers and students to collaborate, together we can ensure that schooling is relevant, engaging and successful for 21st-century young people.

Making a difference | 13

... the schools of the Knowledge Society will be as different from the schools of the Industrial Society as the medieval market town was different from the industrialized super-city of the Twentieth Century.

Beare, 2002

Is there a stage when we should become angry about complacency in schooling? If there is, then it should be now. We are half a decade into the 21st century and most schools still have structures and curriculum that would be easily recognised back in 1950. We must move beyond paying lip service to the new world of the global knowledge economy and the new world of young people. Knowledge era schooling requires transformation in school culture, teaching behaviours and classrooms.

We know that while there have been a large number of changes in school curricula, innovations in classroom teaching methods and in using technology, schools have not changed much. We can clearly see the strong similarities between schools and classrooms in 2005 and 1955. We know that such schooling is no longer relevant to young people and their world or indeed, to our world and us.

This chapter will look at the position of parents, educators and governments. This book has already focused on the 'voice' of young people. However, if their 'voice' is to be heard appropriately and adequately to make a difference for them, we need to recognise that systemic transformation will only come from adults making deliberate decisions about how their 'adult world' is going to respond to the needs of young people and their 21st-century world. This is not an adult world of public versus private or resourcing, or about divisions in society. It is about what adult people can do to generate schooling and learning experiences that will empower young people to learn and succeed with their new world. If we could learn one further thing from business management literature it might well be about the importance of collaboration within and across schooling.

Parents

As parents, we know that we no longer operate in such an industrial world nor do we want our children growing up to be supervised by 'foremen'. We are at an important crossroad in our life–work decisions for our children. We either think strategically for them or take a short-term perspective that will leave schools more akin to training for factory life than creating knowledge workers.

The short-term perspective is to value discipline, good curriculum standards and the best opportunities to obtain the tertiary entrance score to get into the right university. This is the industrial era 'factory' model.

Such a short-term decision, however, should not overlook the questions: Will my son or daughter obtain permanent employment? (The answer is 'Probably not.') Will my son or daughter be among the one in five who will drop out of tertiary study or among the two in five who will make the wrong course choice and seek to change and take longer at university or TAFE to obtain that primary qualification?

More important questions, however, are whether your sons or daughters will be able to take on the complex challenges and enormous opportunities of the knowledge world or whether they will be locked into a traditional world and a traditional mindset and lost opportunity.

Parents also need to consider the question of transition. Once we talked in terms of 'transition from school to work', but this is no longer relevant. Life–work transition involves the period of both post-compulsory education (senior schooling) and traditional post-school education (university and vocational training). During this period most young people already are involved in study, forms of vocational training (often on the job), part-time/casual employment and very active social lives. Schooling needs to recognise and embrace this period.

This book has tried to create a perspective on how the world has been transformed over the past five to ten years and to illustrate the general failure of 20th-century industrial schooling to come to terms with the new world of the 21st century—the world that our young people are growing up in very quickly!

A call to action
Parents need to:

- Demand that schools will meet the needs of their sons and daughters to link them with the global knowledge economy and help them to develop the disposition and skills to confront the challenges and opportunities of the new world.
- Recognise that we require a highly educated and skilled population of knowledge workers who understand and respect each other. If ever we are to demonstrate a belief in the egalitarian society of Australia, it is now through education.

A prestigious university degree will mean very little if the graduate is unable to adapt and be part of the challenge and opportunity of change. In seeking schooling that will help your sons and daughters become successful self-managers with the disposition and skill to be self-directed life-long learners, you are providing them with the opportunity to achieve their personal goals, not just in short-term post-school study but in the rest of their lives.

Therefore, we need a community of parents who are realistic about the new world, who recognise that schools have to play a major role in helping young people succeed in it and who are prepared to articulate it. These are the parents who will not accept the deaf ears of governments, schools and tertiary institutions, but will demand schooling relevant to the knowledge era and their children.

The strategic perspective asks parents to:

- look at the new knowledge world and its projections for the future
- recognise that their sons and daughters will have many, many career changes in a lifetime that may span about 100 years
- recognise that most will be small business people and independent contractors
- understand that young people will live and work around the globe, and will have to confront, far more than we did, the realities of an inequitable world.

Parents need to make a difference now. Schools are victims of their history: they have traditionally not changed very much and so there are few models for current schools to follow. They fear unleashing the talents of young people; they fear giving them greater freedom and authority; they fear lack of control over young people; they fear parent disapproval over lack of discipline. Change would put these things at risk.

Parents have a powerful voice. They can choose to keep their sons and daughters divorced from the realities of their world and simply focus on tertiary entrance scores, discipline and uniform, or they can refuse to accept the excuses of schools for not engaging their sons and daughters in relevant schooling and within a culture that embraces them as partners in learning.

Parents need to start asking schools for hard information.

- How do you know my child's talents and how do you design an education program for my child?
- What does your school do to engage my child in learning?
- How do you teach for self-directed learning?
- How can you ensure that my child will want to come to school and will continue to love learning?
- What real experiences do you provide in a school day for my child to begin to learn about self-management?
- How do you set expectations with teachers and young people?
- What do you do to help young people manage their social behaviour and prevent anti-social behaviour? Do you still use detentions?

- How do you teach for emotional intelligence (EQ)?
- Will you help my child become resilient?
- How does your life–work counsellor/career counsellor work to help my child understand the future of living, working and learning?
- What outcomes can I expect for my child from this school, in addition to her or his achieving traditional results? I take these for granted.
- Are you still into pastoral care or has your care program changed to teach for self-care, self-management and personal reflection?
- How do you provide the greatest possible freedoms for my son or daughter to learn to be self-directed or have you allowed 'duty of care' to prevent these opportunities?
- Do you have other trained people to provide supervision of your young people so that your teachers can focus on helping my child learn?
- Will your teachers report directly to my child and me so that we can have a partnership in learning?
- Can we communicate immediately and as is needed?

Parents will think of many more questions. However, if they want a school that thinks and acts long term for their child they will start to ask the questions that will identify whether or not the school is a knowledge era school. Parents are now in an era in which they can really make a difference for their sons and daughters.

Australian of the Year, burns specialist Dr Fiona Wood spoke at 'Hear it From the BOSS' in Melbourne early in 2005.

> My father was down a coalmine at 13, and he drummed it into us kids that, if you get up in the morning and you enjoy what you do, you're ahead of the game. So he spent the whole of his life ensuring that his kids had choice. I think really we need to start right back at the beginning in education and say, 'Well, you know, what is special about you? What is it that really makes you tick? What makes you burn? What's your passion?' And from the very beginning make people believe that each special thing within them is worthy of expressing so that when they come into the workforce they are in a position to trade more than just their hours, their hands ... they're in a position to make a choice.

Parents need to ignite this passion for the many talents that their children bring to schooling. Don't let schools fail them in the 21st century.

Educators

Roberto Carniero (2000) reminds us why we need to ask these questions:

> Human beings have been designed for learning. Children come fully equipped with an unassailable drive to explore and experiment rather than conservatively to avoid mistakes. Conversely, our primary institutions of education have been designed to teach

and to control. The same reasoning applies to our prevailing systems of management, which are quite frequently eager to reward mediocre obedience and rote conformity to norms.

In the main, much of the responsibility will rest with school principals and other school leaders to provide the leadership, vision and the school culture that will empower teachers with the freedoms to develop and use their skills with young people. They need to provide the freedom for teachers to own their jobs and to become innovators and risk-takers in their work with young people.

In this knowledge world, the only real asset that a school has is its intellectual asset, primarily its staff, but also its students and parents. Principals have to nurture and invest in them, and motivate them into making a difference. This means that the principal is not a source of authority and control, but a leader with the vision and strategies for change who can then create a collaborative environment for sharing the vision and implementing it.

The greatest challenge facing a principal is one of leadership for the future. This poses complexities and involves risk-taking. The challenge is to alter community, student, teacher, and parent expectations. Principals, particularly in the public and Catholic sectors, can realise the enormous power of their networks by collaborating to demand support for transformation from their departments and governments.

This assumes that school leaders are maintaining their own learning, that they are recognising the global transformation that has taken place, including the changed world of young people, and are prepared to continue as leaders rather than giving up in the face of government and bureaucratic interference.

Principals cannot be lone players. They have to partner and network, create teams inside and outside the school that will work together to realise vision within the confines of limited resources. However, school principals, as change leaders, will need to be autocrats in terms of the vision and strategic policy. These are not issues for consensus in the short to medium term. Once a knowledge era culture is established, then school consensus will be a reality.

The situation also requires teachers who are prepared to:

- take the quantum leap to become professionals
- own their jobs
- work collaboratively with young people
- demand that their associations and unions become professional bodies and assume a different role in supporting them (Beare, 2002)
- be change leaders
- always search for innovative ways to maximise the learning opportunities for young people
- create the fun and engagement of learning
- recognise that as effective teachers they control their own careers and can help bring about knowledge era transformation in their classrooms and schools.

It is not an easy transformation. We have learned, for example, that aligning with the vision is the easy part. However, translating this into practice and obtaining commitment to the changes is difficult. So much of the translation into practice is contrary to what presently exists and all the accumulated experience we have about what schools and teachers do.

What we also have learned is that the most difficult area of the transformation is the sharing of authority and dealing with issues that are traditionally associated with discipline. In this, teachers need a lot of support.

We, as leaders, need to know our teachers' capabilities, dispositions, their issues with and approaches to learning so that we can plan for and work with them as individuals. We have to be able to practise in our supportive relationships with them what we are asking them to practise in their teaching. This includes holding them accountable and having appropriate consequences for those who won't work with a 21st-century vision for the future. We demand teachers do this for young people and we must model it with them.

Teachers also need space and time to fly with new freedoms. They need to know that it is okay to make mistakes and that they do not have supervisors sitting over every move. If we want innovators, then they need to feel the confidence to admit, 'This didn't work: I need to look at another way.' This is not experimenting, but rather using our sagacity (Caldwell, 2004)—using our accumulated knowledge and wisdom to do things differently.

Perhaps it is time to replace the term 'teacher' with 'educator'. In doing this we might then begin to reflect on what learning is and how people learn. In earlier chapters, I referred to literature about early learning. We need to 'get over' the belief that secondary learning is both more important and very different from early learning. Simply because the end of schooling culminates in assessment for university entrance, many have the belief that this is the key point. This is only dictated by the universities. It could be Year 9 literacy testing, for example! We need to recognise that the higher education system distorts the value of schooling and real schooling outcomes by demanding that these outcomes be converted into a tertiary entrance score that makes student selection easier for them. This score has absolutely nothing to do with schooling except that we have allowed the media and sometimes politicians to get away with using this score as a standard against which to judge schools. It is a sad reflection on how much we value university education above all other forms of education and training when only 30 per cent of students go to university and, in fact, the other 70 per cent create much of the country's economic value.

If I were to put the essence of this book into the context of learning theory I would first argue the case for eclecticism in that the world of 21st-century knowledge era learning is too complex to be encased within particular learning theories. Professor Brian Caldwell (2004) reminds us of 'sagacity' where effective educators adapt their vast accumulation of knowledge and experience to the new context of schooling for the knowledge era.

Second, I would suggest that we have much to learn from the scaffolding notion highlighted by Vygotsky (Berk and Winsler, 1995). Scaffolding is the complex and delicately choreographed dance between the student and the teacher from the start of schooling through to the final years. This is complemented in the Reggio Emilia approach to early learning:

> ...learning is the key factor on which a new way of teaching should be based, becoming a complementary resource to the child and offering multiple options, suggestive ideas, and sources of support. Learning and teaching should not stand on opposite banks and just watch the river flow by; instead, they should embark together on a journey down the water. Through an active, reciprocal exchange, teaching can strengthen learning how to learn.
>
> Edwards, Gandini and Forman, 1998: 83

From the early years and throughout learning, the development of the skills for and the disposition towards self-directed learning in a community of collaboration stands as central to what young people need to 'deal effectively with the present' as the key component to preparing them for the future (Eisner Solidus 2003/04).

Teacher educators and researchers also need to recognise that they have important roles in leading the way and providing ideas and directions. Implications exist for both pre-service and in-service teacher education. Neither is responding well to the transformational needs of the 21st century. The research focus should move to the more strategic issues of schooling and its purposes and the relationship between schooling and the global knowledge economy. Schooling outcomes need to be challenged through both research and teacher education. Clearly, research and development efforts need to be directed towards the major non-academic outcomes from schooling: how do we assess and report on self-management? How do we teach for, assess and report on the development of emotional maturity (EQ), resiliency? How do we assess and report on self-directed learning? How do we effectively teach for the disposition to learn and not just the academics of learning? If we are seeking disposition towards and skills for life-long learning through schooling, how do we teach for it, assess it and report on it? Researchers and teacher educators need, for example, to move from the cosy confines of researching literacy and numeracy to death in a technological society, researching social class when young people have moved closer together through technology despite their backgrounds, researching classrooms when they have become even more outdated and so on.

Researchers need to start asking better questions about young people and their knowledge world.

Beare's (2001) Angelica asked,

> So, do you know what to teach me? Do you know what I need to learn? And do you know how to teach me? Are you confident that you can design a curriculum which will equip me to live in my world?

Researchers should be exposing young teacher trainees to sagacity and to the eclecticism that can come from exposing theory (Vygotsky, Reggio Emelia and others) to the realities of young people, their schools and the 21st century. Again, like their school counterparts, those training secondary teachers should look at what is happening in early learning and ask: If it can occur with four-year-olds, why not sixteen-year-olds?

Education academics and teachers in schools need to engage in identifying, trying and assessing practical steps that will assist teachers to deal with the new world of young people. Too much attention is given to the issues of behaviour management and discipline, particularly in in-service programs and pre-service teaching practices. These issues create a negative culture and a negative mindset. We all know that if a single behaviour problem keeps occurring it sets up a negative feeling and soon, a class is branded, despite the fact that all but a few are engaged positively. Teacher education and the practical experiences provided for trainee teachers need to expose the wonders, opportunities and achievements in working with young people.

So, at both a school and individual teacher level, attention needs to be given to how we create a culture of engagement and working together. With the introduction in most Australian states of new curriculum directions—for example, the Victorian Essential Learning Standards—there is an opportunity to remove familiar content and process from all years up to the final two or three, so as to allow teachers to explore new approaches.

At a time when schools need to become innovative, take risks and explore all the opportunities for a knowledge era learning environment, there are governments demanding greater forms of traditional accountability. How many schools will attempt a new culture in the middle years when the federal government is intent on introducing a performance and very public testing regime at Year 9, testing for traditional 20th century outcomes? Already the media, schools and parents are talking about teaching for these tests and the public 'report cards' that will emerge. No teacher will feel comfortable in being innovative unless their whole school commits to change. How many teachers will feel comfortable when in their own states what is recognised by authority is traditional academic success in Year 12 outcomes? Authorities still have not attuned to the 21st century's needs for self-managing, self-directed learners.

Teachers are very capable of taking practical steps to make a difference in their teaching–learning relationships with young people. Much of this book suggests that we need to start with the teaching profession so that teachers, as educators, can step beyond their experiences that suggest 'that educational ideas and practices can derive only from official models or established practices' (Edwards, Gandini and Forman, 1998: 57).

Teachers can be helped to make the transition to the 21st-century knowledge era. However, they need a culture that empowers it. The first step to change, therefore, is a commitment from schools that there is a need for schooling transformation. The second step is to create a culture where people, both younger and older, are able to take risks and make mistakes. Part of this culture also is government, media and community commitment to a culture that empowers schools to make a difference for young people.

Government

We need governments and political parties that will provide leadership and vision. Governments need to:

- Acknowledge that schooling is for young people and their interaction with living and working both now and for their futures.
- Seek policy advice that is not politically driven but motivated by realistic assessments of the global knowledge economy and what sort of labour market nations need to be competitive.
- Realistically assess what our young people need from schooling, what attitudes and capabilities they need if they are to take up the opportunities of the new world.
- Look at inequalities in relation to communication and information technologies and recognise that the costs of helping all families with children under 15 years of age to have home access to the Internet will not be prohibitive. Knowledge era schooling recognises that it is important for young people and their parents to have access to the Internet because it is today's major source of information.
- Establish a national framework and create lighthouse projects for knowledge era schooling.
- Create, within such a framework, support for national and international networking between schools.
- Move away from the divide of private versus public, wealthy private versus the rest and look at how we should be part of an urgent networking priority to create schooling relevant to the 21st century and its young people.
- Assume a strategic leadership role for schooling.
- Recognise that we need innovation more than accounting (literacy tests are simply accounting measures).
- Support research effort into schooling and the relationship between schooling and the global knowledge economy.

Despite our national economic health and good growth, we should realise that we do not have the luxury of time, as our current wealth is more consumption based than cemented in knowledge creation. Look at how much of our traditional wealth base has collapsed or gone to the larger and cheaper workforces overseas. Other smaller countries have managed substantial transformations to create a knowledge economy labour market and national economy (Ireland, Israel, Malaysia, Singapore, Hong Kong, South Korea, Sweden, Norway). We need to keep up and direct leadership and resources to our schooling system. Knowledge workers cannot simply be a product of universities or technical colleges. They need to come from schooling. We need to recognise that the United States, China and the major European countries have much larger populations and have time to transform their schooling systems. They only need a much smaller proportion of their populations to be innovative, entrepreneurial knowledge workers. They still need a much broader range of workers to manage their greater economic diversity, meet their own consumption needs and provide the rest of the world with both knowledge and manufactured product. Australia does not have the population to afford such a luxurious position.

In this book I have tried to demonstrate an imperative and suggest a need for urgent transformation of our schools. The issue seeks strategic commitment from governments and an endeavour to move away from high profile immediate issues, such as discipline in secondary schools, increased literacy funding, private versus public. If governments can do this, then their departments may find better longer-term solutions rather than spending their time on 'big brother' interventions in schools to maintain a sense of systemic control.

Australian governments can learn from the experiences of the Blair government in the United Kingdom and its Specialist Schools Trust, which has created a culture for student-focused change in secondary schools. The UK government has set up a culture in which change is possible and where, in fact, teachers and school leaders are comfortable with change being part of their workplace. They have the potential now, therefore, to take their schools from the 20th-century industrial world to the 21st-century knowledge world and create knowledge era schooling. Australia doesn't have this culture … yet.

Conclusion

None of us in schools would deny that the world has changed and is rapidly changing. We all recognise that there are negatives. But negatives have always been associated with change. However, these negatives aside, young people are different and their world is permanently changed. They are no longer simply going through a phase of development like previous generations. They are of this new world.

One can ponder the question: Just how much do young people need our schools? The answer is that they do need schooling, but not our industrially managed 20th-century schools. They need schools that will respect their talents, work with them, provide learning experiences that converge living and working through both curriculum and exposure to the rich world outside of school, provide and value learning experiences for emotional intelligence, and which facilitate young people being able to self-manage, not simply pass teacher-directed assessments.

Twenty-first century schooling relies on:

- sharing knowledge creation and authority with young people
- a culture that allows young people to take risks: to have space, time and the freedom to explore

- a culture of change where young people are able to develop resiliency, adaptability and personal flexibility to become not only people who can cope with change but also agents of it
- modelling the world in which young people live and in which they will work
- acknowledging that intelligence extends beyond the academic disciplines and includes multiple intelligences and individual talents that can operate in a social, collaborative sense, converging academic and vocational curricula
- knowledge era teaching and learning skills. These include:
  - ¬ collaboration and teaming
  - ¬ sharing leadership
  - ¬ negotiating to arrive at shared expectations
  - ¬ engagement management (managing learning rather than classrooms)
  - ¬ creating and managing knowledge
  - ¬ teaching for self-awareness and self-evaluation
  - ¬ teaching for self-management and self-directed learning.

Eltham College of Education has demonstrated that schooling transformation for the knowledge era is possible in creating a culture of change and adaptability. The knowledge era school ensures that the talents and excitement that young people bring to kindergarten have not been boxed and controlled but have grown exponentially by the time they finish school. They will graduate still excited by learning and, therefore, very capable, adaptable, engaged, sophisticated in a worldly sense and productive life-long learners. They will feel good about themselves and the world that they will manage.

Selected references

AC Nielson Research 1999, on Employer satisfaction with the skills of university and TAFE graduates.

Airasian, P 1997, 'Constructivist cautions', *Phi Delta Kappa*, Feb, vol. 78, no. 6, pp. 444–9.

Allee, V 1997, *The knowledge evolution: expanding organizational intelligence*, Butterworth-Heinemann, Boston.

Ames, Nancy 2003, 'To truly educate', *Principal Leadership*, vol. 3, p. 7.

Aphek, Edna 2001, 'Children of the information age: a reversal of roles', *Turkish Online Journal of Distance Education*, October 2002, vol. 3, no. 4.

Australian Bureau of Statistics 2001, *Census of population and housing*, viewed 19 September 2005, <http://www.abs.gov.au>.

Australian Bureau of Statistics 2004, *Householders' use of information technology*, viewed 19 September 2005, <http://www.abs.gov.au>.

Australian National Training Authority 1997, *The readiness of the VET sector for flexible delivery including on-line learning*, TAFE Queensland.

Australian National Training Authority 1997, *The readiness of the VET Sector for flexible delivery including on-line learning: a guide for developers of curriculum and training packages*, TAFE Queensland.

Australian National Training Authority 1997, *The readiness of the VET sector for flexible delivery including on-line learning: a guide for practitioners*, TAFE Queensland.

Banks, R 1997, *Bullying in schools* (ERIC report no. EDO-PS-97-170), ERIC Clearinghouse, University of Illinois, Champaign.

Barker, K 1998/99, 'Serving the learning needs of education consumers', *Education Canada*, Winter 1998/99, vol. 38, issue 4, p. 25.

Beare, H 2001, *Creating the future schools*, Routledge, UK.

Beare, H 2002, 'The future school: seven radical differences', *Principal Matters*, November, pp. 40–5.

Beare, H and Slaughter, R 1993, *Education for the twenty-first century*, Routledge, London.

Bentley, T 2002, 'Letting go: complexity, individualism and the left', *Renewal*, vol. 10, no. 1.

Berk, L and Winsler, A 1995, *Scaffolding children's learning: Vygotsky and early childhood education*, National Association for the Education of Young Children, Washington DC.

Borg, MG 1999, 'The extent and nature of bullying among primary and secondary school-children', *Educational Research*, vol. 412, pp. 137–53.

Brain, P 1999, *Beyond meltdown: the global battle for sustained growth*, Scribe Publications, Melbourne.

Brockett, RG and Heimstra, R 1990, *Self-direction in adult learning: perspectives on theory, research, and practice*, Croom Helm, London.

Brookfield, S 1984, 'Self-directed learning: a critical paradigm', *Adult Education Quarterly*, vol. 35, pp. 59–71.

Brookfield, S 1985, 'Self-directed learning: a critical review of research'. In S Brookfield (ed.), *Self-directed learning: from theory to practice*, pp. 5–16, Jossey-Bass, San Francisco.

Brookfield, S 1985a, *New directions for continuing education*, Jossey-Bass, San Francisco.

Cain, K 2005, Imaging the future—building the vision. Presented at The Challenge to Re-imagine the school!, iNet Workshop.

Caldwell, B 2004, *Re-Imagining the self-managing school*, Specialist Schools Trust, London.

Caldwell, B 2005, The new enterprise logic in public education. Paper presented at the Sustaining Prosperity: New Reform Opportunities for Australia conference, 31 March–1 April 2005, The University of Melbourne.

Candy, PC 1991, *Self-direction for lifelong learning*, Jossey-Bass, San Francisco.

Carmichael, L 1992, *The Australian vocational certificate training system/employment and skills formation council*, National Board of Employment, Education and Training, Canberra.

Carniero, R 2000, On knowledge and learning for the new millennium. Australian College of Educators, Education 2000 Conference: Priorities for the New Millennium, 2–5 July 2000, Blue Mountains, NSW.

Christie, G 2002, 'Of children and tennis balls', *Thinking Parent*, September, issue 2.

Christie, G, Warner, D and Choy, S 1998, 'The readiness of the vocational education and training client for flexible delivery, including on-line learning'. In proceedings of International Conference on Technology and Education, 8–11 March 1998, Santa Fe.

Christie, G and Warner, D 1999, Distance learning readiness: a cross-cultural comparison. ICTE Edinburgh 1999, Preparation for the New Millennium: Directions, Developments, and Delivery.

Christie, G and Warner, D 1999a, A cross-cultural comparison of readiness for independent learning. Paper accepted for Conference Chiba, Japan, 1999.

Crichton, M 2004, *State of fear*, HarperCollins, Sydney.

Cullum, A 1971, *The geranium on the window sill just died, but teacher you went right on*, Harlin Quist Books, Ohio.

Cuttance P 2001, *Schooling for the knowledge society*, Incorporated Association of Registered Teachers of Victoria IARTV, seminar series no. 107, IARTV, Melbourne.

Davis, S and Meyer, C 1999, *Blur: the speed of change in the connected economy*, Warner Books Education, New York.

Delors, J 1996, Learning: the treasure within. Report to UNESCO of the International Committee on Education for the Twenty-first Century UNESCO Publishing, Paris.

Demos Paper 2005, About learning. Report of the working group, January.

Department of Education, Science and Training 2003, Review report on teaching—Australia's teacher: Australia's future, main report, p. 8.

Department of Employment, Training and Industrial Relations (DEET) 1999, *IT, employment and regional Australia*, Queensland Government.

Dobozy, E 1999, Constructivist and Montessorian perspectives on student autonomy and freedom, Proceedings Western Australian Institute for Educational Research Forum 1999, viewed 19 September 2005, <http://education.curtin.edu.au/waier/forums/1999/dobozy.html>.

Drucker, P 1995, *Post-capitalist society*, Butterworth-Heinemann, London.

Drucker, P 2000, 'Managing knowledge means managing oneself', *Leader to Leader*, Spring 2000.

Education 2000 Trust 1997, A proposal to Prime Minister Tony Blair. Submitted by the Trustees of Education 2000, 21st Century Learning Initiative.

Edwards, C, Gandini, L and Forman G (eds) 1998, *The hundred languages of children: the Reggio Emilia approach—advanced reflections*, Ablex Publishing Corporation, Norwood, NJ.

Eisner, E 2004, 'Preparing for today and tomorrow', *Educational leadership*, December 2003/January 2004.

Elleray, W 2005, *The man in the middle*, Time Warner, UK.

Ellis, B 2002, *Goodbye Babylon*, Penguin, Melbourne.

Emmerton, P 2000, Managing oneself and the future of work. Morgan and Banks workshop papers.

European Commission 1994, *White Paper: Teaching and learning: towards the learning society*, European Communities, Brussels.

European Commission 1996, *Green Paper: Living and working in the information society: people first*, European Communities, Brussels.

Finn, B 1991, *Young people's participation in post-compulsory education and training: report of the Australian Education Council review committee*, Australian Government Publishing Service, Canberra.

Freeman, R 1999, *The economic problem of youth around the world*, viewed 19 September 2005, <http://www.info.gov.hk/cpu/english/papers/e-freemn.rtf>.

Garrison, DR 1997, 'Self-directed learning: Toward a comprehensive model', *Adult Education Quarterly*, vol. 48, no. 1, pp. 18–33.

Glover, D, Gough, G, Johnson, M and Cartwright, N 2000, 'Bullying in 25 secondary schools: incidence, impact and intervention', *Educational Research*, no. 422, pp. 141–56.

Goldfinger, C 1996, The intangible economy and its implications for statistics and statisticians, Eurostat ISTAT Seminar, Bologna.

Goleman, D 2004, 'What makes a leader?', *Best of Harvard Business Review*, Jan. 2004 (reprint 1998).

Goleman, D, Boyatzis, R and McKee, A 2004, *The New Leaders,* Time Warner Paperbacks, London.

Gross, M 2003, 'Does criticising your child's teacher disempower your child?', *Understanding Our Gifted*, Summer 2003.

Grow, GO 1991, 'Teaching learners to be self-directed', *Adult Education Quarterly*, vol. 41, no. 3, pp. 125–49.

Grow, GO 1994, 'In defence of the staged self-directed learning model', *Adult Education Quarterly*, vol. 44, no. 2, pp. 109–14.

Guglielmino, L 1977, Development of the self-directed learning readiness scale, PhD thesis, University of Georgia, Dissertation Abstracts International, 38, 6467A.

Guglielmino, LM and Guglielmino, PJ 1991, *The learning preference assessment*, Organization Design and Development, Inc., King of Prussia, Pennsylvania.

Guglielmino, LM and Guglielmino, PJ 1991a, *The learning preference assessment, trainer guide*, Organization Design and Development, Inc., King of Prussia, Pennsylvania.

Hamel, G 2000, *Leading the revolution,* Harvard Business School Press, Boston.

Hamel, G 2002, *Innovation now*, Fast Company, December, viewed 19 September 2005, <http://www.fastcompany.com/online/65/innovation.html>.

Hamel, G 2003, 'Innovation as a deep capability', *Leader to Leader*, Winter 2003, pp. 19–24.

Hamel, G 2004, Gary Hamel Seminars, Global Leaders Network, Sydney Convention Centre, 7 May 2004.

Hamel, G and Valkangas, L 2003, 'The quest for resilience', *Harvard Business Review*, September 2003.

Handy, C 2001, *The elephant and the flea*, Hutchinson, London.

Hargreaves, D 2003, 'From improvement to transformation', IARTV seminar series, paper no. 122, March.

Hargreaves, D 2004a, *Personalising learning: next step in working laterally*, Specialist Schools Trust, London.

Hargreaves, D 2004b, *Personalising learning 2, student voice and assessment for learning,* Specialist Schools Trust, London.

Hargreaves, D 2005, *Personalising learning 3*, Specialist Schools Trust, London.

Hatcher, TG 1997, 'The ins and outs of self-directed learning', *Training and Development*, February 1997, pp. 35–9.

Herbeson, E 1991, 'Self-directed learning and level of education', *Australian Journal of Community Education*, vol. 31, no. 30, pp. 196–201.

Hesselbein, F and Cohen, PM (eds) 1999, *Leader to Leader,* Jossey-Bass, San Francisco.

Hoffer, E 1973, *Reflections on the human condition*, HarperCollins, New York.

Horne, D 1964, *The lucky country,* Penguin, Sydney.

House of Representatives Standing Committee 2003, Parliamentary enquiry into teaching.

Jackson, P 1968, *Life in classrooms,* Holt, Rinehart and Winston, New York.

Johnson, S 1998, *Who moved my cheese?*, Random House, Sydney.

Knowles, M 1975, *Self-directed learning*, Follet Publishing Co., Chicago.

Knowles, MS 1980, *The modern practice of adult education: from pedagogy to andragogy* 2nd edn, Follet Publishing Co., Chicago.

Latham, M 1998, *Civilising global capital,* Allen & Unwin, Sydney.

Lipnack, J and Stamps, J 1994, *The age of the network: organising principles for the 21st century*, John Wiley and Sons, New York.

Lipnack, J and Stamps, J 1997, *Virtual teams: people working across boundaries with technology*, John Wiley and Sons, New York.

Maglen, L 2001, Australia in the emerging global knowledge economy: changing employment patterns 1986–87 to 1999–2000. Report to ANTA, Monash University, CEET.

Maher, A 2004, The self-managed student. Paper presented at the 12th Specialist Schools Trust National Conference for Affiliated Schools, Birmingham.

Mangan, J 1998, *Non-standard employment in Queensland—an empirical analysis*, Department of Employment, Training and Industrial Relations, Brisbane.

Marx, G 2003, *Ten trends: educating children for a profoundly different future*, ASCD National Conference Online, April.

McCrindle, M 2004, *Understanding generation Y*, The Australian Leadership Foundation, North Parramatta.

McCrindle, M 2004a, *The ABC of XYZ: generational diversity at work*, McCrindle Research Pty Ltd, Cherrybrook, NSW.

McKay-Brown, L and Warner, D 2001, PeaceBuilders®: a prevention process for schools and the communities. Paper presented at Bullying Prevention Conference, Hobart.

Miller, R and Bentley, T 2004, *Possible futures: four scenarios for 21st century schooling,* NCSL, Nottingham.

Morrison, TR 1995, 'Global transformation and the search for a new educational design', *International Journal of Lifelong Education*, no. 14, pp. 188–213.

OECD 1999, *Learning cities and regions,* OECD, Paris.

OECD 2001, *What schools for the future,* Report from the Centre for Educational Research and Innovation, Paris.

Pekrul, S 2004, Student voice: the voices of today and tomorrow. iNet online conference on 'Student voice', viewed 23 October 2005, <http://www.sst-inet.net>.

Peters, T 1994, *The Tom Peters seminar, crazy times call for crazy organisations,* Vintage, New York.

Phillips, M 2005, 'A recent example of how synergy can lead to new models of educational delivery to meet the needs of students', The Challenge to Re-imagine!, iNet Workshop, 17 February.

Power, C 2003, *Towards 2010: Australian education in an international context*, Occasional Paper Series, Australian College of Educators.

Quah, D 1998, 'A weightless economy', *UNESCO Courier*, December.

Quisumbing, L and de Leo, J 2002, 'Values education in a changing world: some UNESCO perspectives and initiatives', in *Australian College of Education College Year Book 2002*, Australian College of Education, Canberra.

Reid, A 2003, *Educating for wisdom,* Occasional Paper Series no. 3, Australian College of Education, Deakin West, ACT.

Rowe, K 2000, 'Exploding the "myths" and exploring "real" effects in the education of boys', *The Boys in Schools Bulletin*, vol. 3, no. 3, pp. 10–16.

Rushkoff, D 1997, *Children of chaos: surviving the end of the world as we know it*, HarperCollins, London.

Salter, C 2001, 'Attention, class!!! 16 ways to be a smarter teacher', Fast Company, issue 53, p. 114.

Savage, C 1996, *Fifth dimension management*, Butterworth-Heinemann, Boston.

Seddon, T and Deer, C (eds) 1992, *A curriculum for senior secondary years*, ACER Press, Melbourne.

Slade, M 2001, 'Listening to the boys', *The Boys in Schools Bulletin*, vol. 4, no. 1, pp. 10–18.

Slade, M 2002, *Listening to the boys*, Shannon Research Press, Adelaide.

Slade, M and Trent, F 2000, 'What the boys are saying: examining the views of boys about declining rates of achievement and retention', *International Education Journal*, vol. 1, no. 3, pp. 201–29.

Smith, L and Cranston, N 1998, *Senior colleges' evaluations*, Queensland Department of Education.

Sveiby, K 1997, *The new organizational wealth: managing and measuring knowledge based assets*, Berrett Koehler, San Francisco.

TAFE Queensland 1997, *Markets, products and delivery for the 21st century*, Brisbane.

Tapscott, D 1998, *Growing up digital: the rise of the next generation*, McGraw-Hill, New York.

Tapscott, D, Lowy, A and Ticoll, D 1998, *Blueprint to the digital economy*, McGraw-Hill, New York.

The Age 2005, 'State school students "on top at uni"', 6 April, Melbourne, p. 7.

The Australian 2004, Schools, 2 August, Melbourne.

The Sunday Age 2005, 'Students a vintage crop when it comes to winemaking', 27 March, Melbourne.

The Herald Sun 2004, VCE Squad, August, Melbourne.

The Herald Sun 2005, Learn, 29 March, Melbourne.

The Times 2004, 'Violence leads to exclusion of 17 000 pupils in one term', 31 July, London, p. 1.

Tough, A 1967, *Learning without a teacher: a study of tasks and assistance during adult self-teaching projects*, The Ontario Institute for Studies in Education, Toronto.

Turkle, S 1995, *Life on the screen: identity in the age of the Internet*, Simon and Schuster, New York.

Warner, D 1987, The distinctive features of experienced teachers thinking about teaching. PhD thesis, University of New England.

Warner, D, Christie, G and Choy, S 1998, Flexible delivery: the readiness of the VET sector. Report to the Australian National Training Authority, TAFE Queensland, Brisbane.

Warner, D and Christie, G 1998, The readiness of tertiary students for flexible learning and online delivery. European Distance Education Network Conference, Bologna.

Warner, D and Christie, G 2000, How effective is school in developing skills for self-directed learning, including use of technology? Education 2000 Conference: Priorities for the New Millennium.

Warner, D and Maher, A 2002, Leading to empower teachers and students: an Australian context, paper presented at the National Middle School Conference, Portland, Oregon, November.

Warner, D and Maher, A 2003, Will schooling fail the knowledge era? AHISA Senior Staff Conference, Hobart, April.

Warner, D and Maher, A 2005, Transforming for the 21st century knowledge era: a case study, IARTV seminar series no. 144.

Wood, F 2005, Hear it From the BOSS Conference, Melbourne.

Wood, D and Middleton, D 1975, 'A study of assisted problem solving', *British Journal of Psychology*, vol. 66, pp. 181–91.